FINANCIAL
GAME PLAN™
FOR COLLEGE STUDENTS

a time of learning

Topaz Consulting, LLC
A Better World Through Financial Education ™

Financial Game Plan™ for College Students

Copyright © 2007 Topaz Consulting, LLC

All rights reserved.

ISBN: 1-4196-4689-3

Library of Congress Control Number: 2006907208

No part of this book may be reproduced in any form without written permission in advance from the publisher.

Inquiries regarding permission for use of the material contained in this book should be addressed to:

BookSurge Publishing
7290 B Investment Drive
North Charleston, South Carolina 29418

Printed in the United States of America

This publication is designed to provide accurate and authoritative information with regard to the subject matter covered. It is sold with the understanding that the publisher is not engaged in rendering legal, accounting, or other professional advice. If legal advice or other expert assistance is required, the services of a competent professional person should be sought.

To order additional copies, please contact:
Topaz Consulting, LLC
www.TopazConsultingLLC.com
books@TopazConsultingLLC.com
or
BookSurge, LLC
1-866-308-6235

A Time of Learning

Your college years are a time of learning, exploring, and growing. Part of your learning experience at college must include personal finance. Using some of the suggestions offered in the ***Financial Game Plan™ for College Students*** can start you on the right path to financial success so that you can achieve the goals you establish during your lifetime.

Consider taking personal finance courses at college to enhance your financial knowledge. Financial knowledge lasts a lifetime and assists in making informed decisions that benefit you and your family.

We wish you the best as you start your journey to financial independence.

Topaz Consulting, LLC
A Better World Through Financial Education™

About the Book

The ***Financial Game Plan™ for College Students*** examines the financial decisions that today's college students are likely to face and offers a straightforward, easily-understood, and practical roadmap for handling each one. Whether you're organizing your financial matters, shopping for student loans, or purchasing your first car, the ***Financial Game Plan™ for College Students*** explains the most efficient, economical steps to take and highlights some of the mistakes to avoid.

Although the ***Financial Game Plan™ for College Students*** will not be the last finance book you will need to buy, it should be one of the first personal finance books you purchase to assist in gaining knowledge about the basic elements of financial transactions.

The ***Financial Game Plan™ for College Students*** does not provide accounting, investment, legal, or tax advice. Nevertheless, this guide can be used by college students as a resource to make better financial decisions and to minimize costly financial mistakes.

Best wishes as you start your journey to financial success.

<u>Topaz Consulting, LLC</u>
A Better World Through Financial Education ™

About the Author

Topaz Consulting, LLC is a consulting company that provides practical and timely financial information to assist individuals in making informed financial decisions that are right for them.

The company's team consists of professionals with backgrounds in accounting, auditing, business management, consulting, editing, education administration, engineering, executive management, graphics design, information technology, law, leadership, marketing, process improvement, project management, publishing, real estate, taxation, teaching, website design, and writing.

The ***Financial Game Plan*™ *for the Young Adult*** was released by Topaz Consulting, LLC in April, 2006 and the ***Financial Game Plan*™ *for Newlyweds*** was released by Topaz Consulting, LLC in October, 2006.

Topaz Consulting, LLC was formed in Sarasota, Florida, with the belief that its work will lead to "A Better World Through Financial Education™."

Table of Contents - Chapters

Chapter	Topic	Page
-	How to Use This Guide	xiii
1	Financial Game Plan	1
2	College Student Financial Checklist	15
3	Consumer Rights and Responsibilities	21
4	Banking Relationship	29
5	Paying Bills	39
6	Savings and Investments	45
7	Financial Applications	59
8	Scholarships, Grants, and Student Loans	67
9	Credit Card Use	77
10	Debt Management	83
11	Insurance	91
12	Car Purchase	107
13	Taxes	117
14	Credit Management	129

15	Identity Theft	141
16	Budgets	149
17	Net Worth Statement	163
18	Financial and Personal Records	171
19	Additional Thoughts	179

Table of Contents - Exhibits

Exhibit	Topic	Page
1A	Example of Goals	9
1B	Example of a Financial Plan	10
1C	Sample List of Assistant Coaches	12
1D	Sample List of Players	13
4A	Checking Account Reconciliation	36
6A	Decision Checklist for Savings	56
11A	Comparison of Insurance Types	104
11B	Insurance Quote Worksheet	106
12A	Annual Car Budget	115
12B	Costs of Purchasing a Car	116
13A	Federal Income Tax Rate Schedules	127
14A	Credit Bureaus	139
16A	Condensed Annual Budget	156
16B	Condensed Monthly Budget	158
16C	Detailed Annual Budget	160

16D	Detailed Monthly Budget	162
17A	Example of a Net Worth Statement	169
18A	Permanent File Index	176

How to Use This Guide

A quick review of the guide will introduce financial topics that college students encounter but may not fully understand. Each chapter covers a broad financial topic and concludes with a summary of Key Points. Most of the chapters have sample exhibits following the Key Points to enhance the understanding of a topic.

Although some of the information may not apply to you while you are in school, the information will be valuable to you as you start your careers in the future. Now is a good time to become familiar with financial terms and options so that when a financial transaction is presented, you will have a basic understanding of the information needed to make an informed decision.

After a quick review of the guide, you should develop a financial game plan as outlined in Chapter One. The exhibits in Chapter One should help you develop your financial game plan.

Chapter Two provides a college student financial checklist outlining some of the financial steps suggested to establish your financial independence as you begin your journey away from home.

An introduction to consumer rights and responsibilities is provided in Chapter Three to assist you in understanding that, even though you are a student, you still have rights as a consumer.

Chapters Four through Twelve give guidance for specific types of financial transactions. For example, Chapter Four offers suggestions regarding the features that you should consider in establishing a banking relationship.

Chapter Thirteen summarizes the various types of taxes, including information on education tax credits. Taxes are a very important part of personal finance and you should become familiar with the U.S. tax system.

Chapters Fourteen and Fifteen provide information regarding credit management and identity theft. These chapters provide guidance on maintaining a good credit rating, as well as ways to avoid identity theft, which is a growing problem.

To help manage finances, Chapter Sixteen provides guidance on budgeting, which helps to monitor monthly activity. Chapter Seventeen provides guidance on the preparation of a net worth statement, which is a financial scorecard at a certain time.

Chapter Eighteen offers information regarding record-keeping. Finally, Chapter Nineteen concludes with some general comments about financial matters. These chapters provide general financial information that applies to all of your financial dealings.

When you are considering a particular financial transaction, this guide can help you understand the requirements of the transaction and the type of information you need to make an informed decision. Making an informed decision about a transaction will result in a savings of both money and time.

CHAPTER ONE

Financial Game Plan

Health and family relationships are the most important aspects of your life. Nevertheless, your personal financial game plan will play a big part in determining the quality of life that you will have. Money will not necessarily make anyone happy, but the lack of money can make life miserable.

Rather than leaving financial decisions to someone else, develop a plan that incorporates your dreams and goals with your ability to earn and save money. No one seems to earn enough money, but how you use the money you earn will help determine the quality of life that you have.

This guide will provide information and tools to assist you in making the most of your earnings so that you can realize your dreams. It is not about becoming a millionaire, although you might become one. It is not about how to make a million dollars by following a secret approach to becoming rich. It is about giving you tools to manage your finances, whatever they may be, so that you can make choices about how you live.

What is a Financial Game Plan? A financial game plan is a plan that starts with your goals and dreams, such as paying bills on time or paying for college. In order to accomplish your goals, you should develop a financial plan, which includes a budget and a savings plan. A financial game plan is one that brings together your personal goals and dreams with your financial resources.

How Do You Develop a Financial Game Plan? As with any sports team, you need to assess where you are, develop goals, develop a plan, assemble a team to accomplish the plan, understand the rules, develop strategies, and review results. Your financial game plan must be flexible and you should review it at least once a year to incorporate any changes that you make in your goals.

Assessment. To currently assess where you are financially, you should request your free credit reports, prepare a net worth statement, and develop a budget. Credit management (as explained in Chapter Fourteen) will assist in reducing borrowing costs. A net worth statement summarizes the value of the things you own (assets) and the amount you owe to others (liabilities). Chapter Seventeen explains how to prepare a net worth statement. A budget will help organize finances and will also give you a good idea of where you are financially. Chapter Sixteen provides guidance on how to develop and monitor a budget.

Goals. Remember, use your finances to provide a better life for you and your loved ones. Decide what is important and then decide what you must accomplish to realize these goals and dreams (pay for college, buy a car, or take a special vacation). Review your goals at least once a year and change them to meet your current needs. Exhibit 1A provides examples of goals.

Plan. Once you know where you are financially (credit report, net worth statement, and budget) and you know what you want to accomplish (goals), you can put together a plan by using the tools in this guide. Basically, decide how much the goal will cost, when you would like to accomplish this goal, and how you will save to pay for this goal. You should update your financial plan at least annually. Exhibit 1B provides an example of a financial plan.

Team – Assistant Coaches. Next, you need to put together a winning team. You will make the final decisions regarding your finances, but you will certainly want to seek the advice and counsel of the assistant coaches – individuals (such as parents, financial aid counselors, bankers, insurance agents, and stockbrokers) who provide you with advice. But, in the end, it is your future that is impacted by your financial decisions.

For example, if you do not satisfy obligations in accordance with their terms, creditors could sell your possessions. Therefore, you must understand the terms of your financial transactions. The chapters in this guide will point out some of the questions to ask the assistant coaches so that you can make informed decisions.

Over time, you may need to change your assistant coaches. You may outgrow some of your current assistant coaches; they no longer can meet your needs. You will probably increase your coaching staff as you increase your wealth and add a Certified Public Accountant (CPA) and attorney. Exhibit 1C provides a sample list of assistant coaches.

Team – Players. Selecting players is very important so that you can get the best results from your game plan. You can have a great game plan and assistant coaches, but if your players don't perform, you will not be successful.

Who are the players? The players in a financial game plan are the organizations that provide services to you. They include banks, credit card companies, lenders, investments, and insurance companies. For example, if you want to be able to pay bills online, you need a bank that provides online bill pay. Exhibit 1D provides a sample list of players.

Rules of the Game. Just as understanding the rules of the game is important in sports, understanding the rules of finance is important for you to maximize your financial results.

For example, in football, tackling the player with the football is the objective when you are on defense. However, tackling the player with the basketball is not a good idea. In fact, you would probably be ejected from the game for such a move in a basketball game.

In finance, paying three points on a home mortgage is a bad financial move; making a three point shot in basketball is fantastic.

In most sports, a higher score is good. Likewise, a higher credit score is good in finance because you will pay less when you borrow money. In golf, a low score is good. When borrowing money, a low interest rate is good.

In sports, you try to minimize penalties. In finance, you want to eliminate any financial penalties, such as prepayment penalties, late payment penalties, early withdrawal penalties, excessive fees, and anything that may cost you more.

Unfortunately, most of the penalties in finance are buried in the "fine print," which, as its name implies, is usually very small print and hard to read. To protect yourself financially, you must be diligent and take the time and effort to read and understand the "fine print" provisions so that you can avoid penalties. If the penalties are excessive, you must move on to another service provider where the terms may be more acceptable.

As you complete this guide, you will become more familiar with the rules of finance, which will assist you in developing your strategies.

Strategies. To maximize your results, you need to develop strategies regarding financial transactions. You can have a great plan, assistant coaches, and players, but still not achieve the desired results because you did not use the right strategies based on the rules of finance. Some financial strategies to consider are listed below.

- "Pay yourself first" is not just a saying, but it is the best way to enjoy your earnings throughout your life.

- Monitor your credit by requesting your free credit reports. Try to maintain a credit rating of good or excellent.

- Shop comparatively for everything. One hundred dollars saved is actually about two hundred dollars earned since you have to pay taxes on your earnings and you incur expenses (such as commuting, clothes, and meals) to earn money. Look for savings when you purchase gas, clothes, loans, autos, homes, insurance, and furniture.

- Minimize small purchases to increase savings for purchases that really make a difference such as a car or home, as well as increase contributions to retirement accounts. Saving just $10 a day results in $3,650 savings a year and $146,000 over 40 years. If an average of 5% were earned on the savings, the savings account would be over $460,000 at the end of 40 years.

- Live within your means; don't mortgage your tomorrow. You might need that loan for something really important.

- Don't forget to give to others. We realize joy by the charitable gifts we make.

- Understand the ongoing cost of a purchase. For example, in addition to the monthly car payment, other costs will include car insurance, state and local car licenses, as well as maintenance costs to operate the car. Similarly, in addition to the monthly mortgage payment, a homeowner will pay homeowner's insurance, property taxes, and utilities (electricity, phone, water, gas, cable, and Internet), as well as maintenance costs for the home.

- Do not over-withhold federal and state income taxes. If you receive a tax refund, you have actually made an interest-free loan to the government. Reduce the tax withheld from your paycheck to the proper amount and invest the additional take home pay in savings that earn interest until you need the money.

- Develop a budget to help you stay on course with your finances. A budget should include your income, savings (remember to pay yourself first), taxes, and monthly expenses.

Results. As mentioned above, you must review your financial game plan at least once a year to assess what you have accomplished and what you need to improve. If you make mistakes, learn from them and move on. Finances are like any other part of life: everyone makes mistakes. Don't spend much time thinking about what you should have done; just learn from any mistakes and move on to accomplishing your goals for the future.

Chapter Sixteen on budgets provides exhibits which compare budget numbers with the actual spending on a monthly basis to help determine whether you are accomplishing goals (budget numbers). Chapter Seventeen provides guidance on preparing a net worth statement which shows where you stand financially at a specific time, such as the end of the year.

Financial Game Plan

Key Points

- Prepare an assessment of where you are – net worth statement and budget

- Develop your goals and dreams

- Prepare a plan to reach your goals and dreams

- Assemble a team of advisors and service providers

- Learn the rules of finance

- Implement strategies to maximize results

    - Pay yourself first; save a portion of every paycheck
    - Shop comparatively for all purchases
    - Live within your means; don't spend more than you can afford
    - Make gifts to help others
    - Understand ongoing costs of a purchase
    - Don't over-withhold income taxes from your paycheck

- Review results

    - Compare budget numbers with actual spending each month
    - Prepare a net worth statement at least once a year

NOTES

Exhibit 1A – Example of Goals

- Pay bills on time

- Pay off credit cards each month

- Save for college expenses

- Maximize college grants

- Maximize college scholarships

- Maintain an excellent credit rating

- Borrow minimum needed for college

- Shop for the lowest interest rate on student loans

- Find a job that fits college schedule

- Buy a car

Exhibit 1B – Example of a Financial Plan

Page 1 of 2

Goal	**When**	**Amount**
Pay off credit cards	Each month	Balance
Pay bills on time	Each month	Balance
Complete FAFSA Form	March, 2007	-
Save for college	Summer job	$3,000
Apply for grants/ scholarships	March, 2007	$2,500
Buy used car	August, 2007	$7,000

Exhibit 1B – Example of a Financial Plan

Page 2 of 2

How to Fund	Where	Comments
From paycheck	Bank account	Monitor credit card purchases
From paycheck	Bank account	Use monthly budget
-	-	Complete as soon as possible
Save $1,000 month during summer job	Savings or money market account	
-	-	Free money
Save $250 month during summer job	Savings or money market account	$750 down and auto loan

Exhibit 1C – Sample List of Assistant Coaches

Profession	**Name**	**Phone**
Parents		
Financial Aid Counselor		
Banker		
Insurance Agent – health		
Insurance Agent – auto		
Insurance Agent – life		
Stockbroker		
Certified Public Accountant (CPA)		
Attorney		

Exhibit 1D – Sample List of Players

Activity	**Company**	**Phone**
Bank account		
Savings account		
Money market account		
Credit card *		
Credit card *		
Insurance – health policy		
Insurance – auto policy		
Insurance – life policy		
Real estate		
Investment accounts		
Auto loan		

* Should not have more than two credit cards

NOTES

CHAPTER TWO

College Student Financial Checklist

As you move to college, you will start a new and exciting chapter in your life where you will have new opportunities and freedoms. But don't forget that you will also have new responsibilities such as paying bills and managing your finances.

This financial checklist will assist you in determining if you have completed the financial steps needed to be successful in living away from home. You may have already completed some of the steps suggested in this guide and can use it to confirm the financial steps taken are the best ones for you. Some steps may require some time to complete and other steps may not apply to you.

Develop a Budget. The most important financial matter for college students is to create a realistic budget which shows the estimated expenses of college and the sources of the money that pay for these expenses. Chapter Sixteen discusses how to prepare a budget and how to use the budget to assist with controlling spending.

Estimate Expenses. Most educational institutions provide the student with an estimate of the cost to attend the college, including tuition, books, and room and board. You will need to decide to either live in a dorm (usually required for freshman students) or to live off campus in an apartment. Most colleges will have meal plans that can be purchased and are necessary if you live in a dorm. Even if you live off campus, a meal plan may be less expensive than preparing and/or buying all of your meals off campus. If you have a car, don't forget to budget for the expenses of operating a car.

Identify Sources of Funds for College Expenses. In addition to money provided by your family and part-time jobs, money is available from scholarships, grants, and student loans as explained in Chapter Eight. Remember that scholarships and grants do not have to be repaid, but student loans will need to be repaid. Therefore, take the time to apply for all scholarships and grants for which you qualify.

Establish Checking Account. You will need to establish a checking account so that you can pay your bills. If you are borrowing money from a bank, you probably should use this bank to establish your checking account. It is important to have a bank that is convenient to you at both college and home, if possible. Chapter Four provides more information on establishing a banking relationship.

Pay Your Bills. Even though you are a student with many deadlines for class work, you must pay your bills on time to avoid expensive late charges and to develop a good credit rating which will be very valuable when you graduate. Your credit rating may even affect your ability to find a job after graduation. Chapter Five provides guidance on the best ways to pay bills.

Minimize Credit Card Use. Although using a credit card is a convenient way to purchase items and pay certain bills, students can quickly get into financial trouble by using credit cards. You should monitor the balance on your credit card during the billing cycle and you should pay the entire credit card balance each month to avoid expensive interest charges. Chapter Nine provides strategies to use regarding credit cards.

Purchase Insurance. Two key types of insurance for college students are health and auto insurance. If you are a full time student, you may be covered by your parents' health insurance policy. If you are not a full time student or your parents do not have health insurance, you may be able to purchase an inexpensive health plan through your college.

If you have a car, you must have auto insurance. Again, if you are a full time student, your car insurance may be included on your parents' auto insurance policy. If your car is not on your parents' auto insurance policy, then you must purchase auto insurance as explained in Chapter Eleven.

Pay Income Taxes. If you are full time student, your parents may claim you as a dependent on their income tax return which should result in income tax savings for your parents. Also, the federal tax law permits up to $2,000 per year in education tax credits for students which may be available to your parents if they claim you as a dependent on their income tax return. Chapter Thirteen provides information on education tax credits.

If your parents do not claim you as a dependent and you have income, you may be required to file income tax returns. You may qualify for federal education tax credits (up to $2,000 per year) to assist with your college expenses. Tax return requirements and education tax credits are explained in Chapter Thirteen.

Avoid Identity Theft. Unfortunately, identity theft applies to students just like everyone else. You must be very diligent in protecting your personal financial information to avoid identity theft as pointed out in Chapter Fifteen.

Keep Records. Now is good time to start practicing good record-keeping. Chapter Eighteen provides guidance on financial and personal records.

TOPAZ CONSULTING, LLC

NOTES

College Student Financial Checklist

KEY POINTS

- Develop a budget

- Estimate college expense

    - Tuition and books
    - Housing – dorm or apartment
    - Food – college meal plan and/or purchased meals
    - Auto expense
    - Recreation and personal expenses

- Arrange for funding of college expenses

    - Family
    - Job
    - Scholarship
    - Grant
    - Student loan

- Establish checking account

- Pay bills on time

    - Avoid late charges
    - Build good credit rating

- Minimize credit card use

  - Monitor charges during billing cycle
  - Pay entire balance each month

- Purchase insurance

  - Health – perhaps on parents' health plan
  - Auto – perhaps on parents' auto insurance plan

- Pay income taxes if necessary

  - Parents may claim as dependent, if full time student
  - May qualify for education tax credit – up to $2,000 per year

- Avoid identity theft

  - Protect financial information

- Keep records

  - Good time to start record-keeping system

CHAPTER THREE

Consumer Rights and Responsibilities

Up to now, your parents have probably taken care of major consumer transactions and you have not needed to understand your rights and responsibilities as a consumer. As you become more independent, it becomes more important for you to understand these rights and responsibilities. This chapter will highlight some of the laws which provide your consumer rights and also point out some of your responsibilities as a consumer.

Educate Yourself. Your first responsibility is to educate yourself about your consumer rights. You can't know if your rights have been violated unless you understand what those rights are. This chapter covers some of your consumer financial rights and other chapters provide guidance on what to expect in a particular financial transaction.

For example, Chapter Ten on debt management explains the different costs associated with a loan. Chapter Twelve discusses the process of buying a car.

Compare Offers. A second responsibility is to be diligent about your financial affairs and shop for the best deal possible. Even though a particular transaction may not violate your rights, you may end up paying too much for the service provided.

For example, credit card companies must disclose the interest rate charged on unpaid balances. If they disclose that the interest rate is 24%, they are in compliance with the law and your rights have not been violated. However, there are many credit card companies that will charge a much lower interest rate on unpaid balances. You should compare credit card interest rates and select the credit card with the lowest interest rate.

Review Documents. Another responsibility is to read all the documents regarding a financial transaction. Some of the financial documents are very long and contain pages of "fine print." Take the time to read the entire document and be sure that you understand the terms of the document. Generally, you will have no right to challenge any term that has been disclosed in the document.

For example, a furniture company offers to sell you furniture and not charge you any interest for one year. The sales agreement states on page 5 in "fine print" that the interest at 24% is deferred for one year. This means that you are charged interest at 24% from the day of purchase, but that you don't have to write a check to pay that interest until one year after purchase. Therefore, your furniture purchase just cost you 24% more than you thought. Your rights have not been violated because the sales agreement clearly states that the interest was deferred rather than not being charged.

Be Honest. A fourth responsibility is to be truthful in all financial dealings. If false statements are made on applications, the transaction may be voided by the company relying on the application. For example, your insurance may be cancelled if information on the insurance application is incorrect.

Pay Obligations as Promised. One of the more important responsibilities you have as a consumer is to pay your obligations as promised. Whether you are making payments on a loan or are paying your monthly utility bills, you must pay the amount due by the due date. Therefore, you must be diligent not to overspend so that you can make your payments as required. If you move, you must notify companies you deal with of your new address so that you can receive your bills on time.

Know the Equal Credit Opportunity Act. This act prohibits discrimination against an applicant for credit because of age, sex, marital status, religion, race, color, national origin, or receipt of public assistance. If credit is denied, the law requires that you be notified in writing of the denial. You may request the reason for the denial be provided to you in writing within 60 days.

Know the Fair Credit and Charge Card Disclosure Act. Financial institutions, retail stores, and private companies must disclose the annual percentage rate, annual fees, and grace periods. This information must be provided with credit card applications and pre-approved credit card solicitations.

If your credit card is used without your permission, you may be held responsible for up to $50 per credit card. You can't be held responsible for any unauthorized charges if you report the credit card lost before it is used. However, if a thief uses your credit card before you report it missing, the most you will owe for unauthorized charges is $50.

Know the Fair Credit Reporting Act. This law establishes procedures for correcting mistakes on a person's credit record and requires that a consumer's record can be used only for legitimate business needs. If you are denied credit, you may request a cost-free credit report within 30 days of the credit denial. Further, this law requires that your credit record is kept confidential.

Know the Fair Debt Collection Practices Act. A debt collector may not engage in any conduct which harasses, oppresses, or abuses any person in connection with the collection of a debt. A debt collector may not use any false, deceptive, or misleading representation in connection with the collection of any debt. Further, a debt collector may not use unfair or unconscionable means to collect or attempt to collect any debt.

Know the Fair Housing Act. This law prohibits discrimination on the basis of race, color, sex, religion, handicap, familial status, or national origin in the financing, sale, or rental of housing.

Know the Truth in Lending Act. This act requires disclosure of the finance charge and the annual percentage rate on loans so that consumers can compare the prices of credit from several sources.

Know the Electronic Fund Transfer Act. This law limits the consumer's liability for unauthorized electronic fund transfers. It also provides consumer protection for all transactions using a debit card or electronic means to debit or credit an account.

Another reason to be diligent about your accounts is to limit your liability for unauthorized electronic fund transfers. If you notify the financial institution within two business days of learning that your card has been lost or stolen, your liability will not be more than $50 for unauthorized transfers of funds. However, if you notify the financial institution more than two days after learning that the card was lost or stolen, your liability is increased to $500 for unauthorized transfers of money.

If a periodic statement shows an unauthorized transfer, you must notify the financial institution within 60 days after the periodic statement was sent; otherwise, you will have unlimited liability for all unauthorized transfers made after the 60-day period. You must reconcile your accounts at least monthly so that you can determine whether you have any unauthorized transfers or charges.

Understand the Complaint Filing Process. You should contact the financial institution first to attempt to resolve the complaint. If the complaint is not resolved with the financial institution, you should contact the institution's regulatory agency for assistance.

Contact the Federal Trade Commission. Your rights as a consumer are protected through numerous laws and regulations at the federal and state level. For additional information on consumer rights or to file a complaint, you should visit the Federal Trade Commission website at www.ftc.gov.

Summary. This chapter provides summary information regarding very complex laws. You should verify that the rules summarized above apply to your situation and that you have a complete understanding of the detail rules before proceeding in any financial transaction.

TOPAZ CONSULTING, LLC

NOTES

Consumer Rights and Responsibilities

Key Points

- Key consumer responsibilities

  - Educate yourself regarding your financial rights
  - Shop before you buy or borrow
  - Review all documents in detail; read the "fine print"
  - Be honest in all dealings
  - Pay all obligations as promised

- Key consumer rights

  - Discrimination is not permitted in lending or housing
  - Disclosure of financial terms is required
  - Reason for credit denial must be given in writing
  - Free credit report must be provided if denied credit
  - Financial information must be kept confidential
  - Liability from stolen or lost credit cards is limited to $50
  - No harassment, abuse, false statements, or unfair practices are permitted in the collection of debts
  - Liability for unauthorized electronic funds transfer will be limited if timely notice is given to the financial institution

- If your consumer rights are violated

  - Contact the company first to try to resolve
  - Then, contact the company's regulatory agency
  - Finally, contact the Federal Trade Commission

NOTES

CHAPTER FOUR
Banking Relationship

Selecting a bank to use for a checking account is one of your first financial decisions. Having a good relationship with a bank is important as you continue to build wealth.

A bank can provide checking and savings accounts, certificates of deposit, credit cards, college loans, auto loans, home mortgages, equity lines of credit, and other financial services. Your bank is a good place to start for any of the services listed above to gain information about current rates and procedures. Another financial institution may provide a better product that you ultimately select, but your bank can provide a reference point to start your search. Some of the issues to consider in selecting a bank are outlined below.

FDIC Insurance. The bank should be a member of the Federal Deposit Insurance Corporation (FDIC). The FDIC insures accounts in member banks for up to $100,000. This means that if the bank should not be able to pay the money that you put into the bank account, the FDIC will pay you the money in the account up to the $100,000 limit.

Free Checking. Free checking should be available for your checking account. Be sure that you understand the requirements for free checking. For example, there may be a requirement to maintain a minimum balance in the checking account, which means that the balance cannot go below a set minimum at any time. If the balance in the checking account goes below the minimum balance required, then the bank will assess a monthly maintenance fee (such as $10 for that month).

Another common requirement is that your payroll check must be directly deposited into the checking account. This requirement is actually beneficial if your employer participates in direct deposit because you don't have to get the paycheck and then go to the bank to deposit it.

Checks. With identity theft on the rise, the amount of information that is printed on checks should be limited. Definitely do **not** include your social security number on the checks. Your name and current address should be sufficient information to be printed on the checks.

Consider ordering duplicate checks for your checking account. Duplicate checks provide a copy of your check at the time the check is written, which is useful if the bank does not return cancelled checks with your bank statement. A duplicate check also provides the check information if you forget to write the information on the check register at the time the check is written. Although you may have free checking, some banks do charge for the printing of checks.

Overdraft Protection. Overdraft protection is an important tool to avoid writing bad checks, which results in a bad credit rating, as well as current charges to your checking account. Basically, the checking account links to another account at the same bank where you have the checking account. If the checking account balance should go below zero, money transfers to the checking account from the other account so that checks are paid.

Typically, the checking account links to a savings account, a credit card, or a line of credit with the checking account bank. If the checking account links to a savings account, you are using savings. However, if the checking account links to a credit card or line of credit account, you are actually borrowing money to pay for the checks. Generally, there is no fee for the transfer of money to the checking account. If you use a credit card account or a line of credit account, you will have to pay interest on the amount transferred until you repay the amount transferred to the checking account.

Interest Checking. With interest rates being low at the present time, interest checking is not very important. The key is to avoid bank charges and not worry too much about receiving interest on the checking account balance. Any excess funds in the checking account should be moved to a savings account (see Chapter Six).

Nevertheless, if you can avoid bank charges, then interest checking is a small plus. For example, if a checking account has an average balance of $1,000, you would only earn $10.00 for an entire year at the current interest rate of 1.00% for interest checking. However, with monthly bank fees of $10.00 a month, the bank fees would be $120.00 per year leaving you with a net loss of $110.00 a year. Again, you should avoid the recurring monthly bank charges.

Electronic Banking. You can use automated teller machines (ATMs), debit cards, and computers (electronic banking) to make withdrawals from accounts and to pay bills rather than writing checks.

Generally, a personal identification number (PIN) is required to access electronic services provided by the bank. Do not share your PIN with anyone since this number can be used to access your financial accounts.

ATM Card. The checking account should be with a bank that offers the free use of an Automated Teller Machine (ATM) card, which permits the withdrawal of money and the making of deposits at the ATM machine at any time, even when the bank is closed. The use of this card should be free when used at the bank's ATM machines.

However, there is usually a charge to use another bank's ATM machine. Therefore, check the location for your bank's ATM machines to make sure that they are convenient to your home, school, and place of work.

Debit Cards. Using a debit card to make purchases will result in money being moved from your checking account to the store's account quickly. Therefore, be sure that sufficient funds are in your checking account to cover any purchases with a debit card. Also, be sure to record the debit card purchase on your check register since money is being removed from the checking account by the debit card purchase.

If you pay credit card balances in full each month, you may wish to use a credit card rather than a debit card because money will stay in your checking account until the credit card is paid.

Checking Account Online. With electronic banking, you can use a computer to view checking account information, pay bills, and transfer funds online. You can reconcile the checking account at any time and monitor activity on the checking account, such as automatic payments for utilities or auto loan payments.

Being able to pay bills online is a great time-saver. You can set up companies that are paid regularly (credit card and utilities) on the computer. After logging on to the account, you can make payments online without having to write checks and mail the check and payment coupon. You can transfer funds between accounts by using online banking, which is useful if you have more than one account with the bank, such as checking and savings accounts.

Receiving electronic bills from companies for monthly bills (again credit card and utilities) is another time-saver. With electronic bills, you can click on the bill to review and schedule the time to pay the bill online.

In addition to saving time by paying bills online, you will save the cost of stamps to mail the payment.

Reconciling Your Checking Account. The easiest way to reconcile your checking account is to compare the check register (where you record the checks you write, deposits made, bank fees, interest earned, electronic payments, automatic payments, and any other items that affect your checking account balance) with the bank checking account statement – either online or paper copy. Do this reconciliation at least monthly for each checking account.

As you compare the check register and the bank statement, put a check mark by each item that is on both the check register and the bank statement. Note that checks that were not posted in the prior bank statement may be posted in the current bank statement and place a check mark now by the check on the check register.

Write on the check register all the items that appear on the bank statement that are not on the check register and put a check mark by each of these items on both the check register and the bank statement. For example, you do not know bank fees and interest earned normally until the monthly cut off date of the bank statement (when the bank stops recording transactions for a particular month). Therefore, write in the bank fees and interest earned on the check register before finishing the checking account reconciliation. Now all the items on the bank statement should have a check mark beside them.

On the back of the bank statement is a form to use to complete the reconciliation. Write in the ending bank statement checking account balance on the form. Add all of the deposits on the check register that are not on the bank statement. Subtract all checks or payments (electronic and automatic payments) on the check register that are not on the bank statement. This balance should equal the balance on the check register. Exhibit 4A provides a sample checking account reconciliation.

Bank Statements. As part of a financial record-keeping system, bank statements should be retained for at least seven years.

Banking Relationship
Key Points

- Your bank should be a member of FDIC

- Checking account should not have monthly fees

- Do not put your social security number on printed checks

- Order duplicate checks for your checking account

- Have overdraft protection by linking your checking account to another account

- Maintain minimum balance to avoid monthly fees

- Use electronic banking

    - Protect your PIN
    - Use your ATM card at only your bank's ATMs to avoid charges
    - Remember that using a debit card moves money out of the checking account quickly
    - Save time with online banking

- Reconcile the checking account monthly

- Keep bank statements for at least seven years

TOPAZ CONSULTING, LLC

Exhibit 4A – Checking Account Reconciliation

Page 1 of 2

1. Compare the bank statement with your check register.

A. Put a check mark by each item on the bank statement and on your check register listed on both the bank statement and on your check register.

B. Add all items on the bank statement that do not have a check mark to your check register. Examples of these items include bank charges, automatic payments, interest earned, and cash withdrawals. Put a check mark by these items on both the bank statement and on your check register.

C. At this point, all items on the bank statement should have a check mark.

2. Enter the bank statement balance at the end of the bank statement period on the bank statement reconciliation form (see next page).

A. Enter on the bank statement reconciliation form all of the deposits on the check register that do not have a check mark. Add these to the bank statement balance. (You will not have any of these items if you do not enter a deposit in your check register until you have deposited the item in the bank.)

B. Enter on the bank statement reconciliation form any charges on the check register that do not have a check mark. Subtract these items from the bank statement balance. Generally, these items will be outstanding checks (checks that you have written which have not cleared the bank).

C. After adding the deposits and subtracting the outstanding checks, the balance on the bank statement reconciliation form should equal the balance on your check register.

Exhibit 4A – Checking Account Reconciliation

3. Sample bank statement reconciliation form:

Bank statement balance		595.29
Add deposits on the check register that are not on the bank statement		
Deposit	0	
Deposit	0	
Total deposits		0
Sub-total		595.29
Subtract checks on the check register that are not on the bank statement		
Check 1092	10.91	
Check 1094	25.32	
Check 1097	19.01	
Total outstanding checks		- 55.24
Account balance		540.05
Check register balance		540.05
Difference (should be zero)		0

NOTES

CHAPTER FIVE
Paying Bills

Your credit rating is very important to everything you attempt to do in life. Whether you are renting an apartment or purchasing a home, your credit rating matters. When you try to have utilities connected, the company will consider your credit rating. If you hope to have a credit card, purchase a car on credit, or search for a job, your credit rating will be important. Not only does your credit rating matter when obtaining credit, it matters when the bank determines the interest rate. The lower the interest rate, the lower the payments and the more money you will have to save or spend on other things.

Paying bills on time is one of the best ways to keep a good credit rating. If at all possible, pay bills ten days before they are due to avoid the possibility of late payment. Not only does paying on time help your credit rating, but you avoid those expensive late payment fees, which take money away from other things you would like to buy.

Checks. Writing checks is one of the most time-consuming ways to pay bills. Not only do you have to write the check, but you have to mail the check with the payment coupon. Your account number should be included on the check so that the company can credit your account for the payment (except credit cards – include only the last four numbers, see Chapter Fifteen on identity theft).

Payment with Your Credit Card. In addition to paying for current purchases (such as gas, clothes, and restaurants), paying monthly bills with a credit card is a good way to avoid late payment fees because the payment is made automatically. You do not need to have cash in the checking account to make this payment. However, you must have cash in the checking account to pay the credit card balance when it is due to avoid interest charges. Do not pay a fee for this service. If there is a fee involved, select another payment method.

Automatic Payments from Your Checking Account. This is also a good way to pay routine monthly payments. Be sure that funds are in the checking account at the time of the payment to cover the charge. It is better to pay bills that are the same amount each month (such as auto loan payments and insurance payments) so that you know the amount that will be charged against the checking account.

Be sure to enter these payments on the check register so that you can verify that the money needed to pay these bills will be in the account. A good way to accomplish this is to enter all automatic monthly payments on the check register on the first of each month, even if they are due later in the month. If there is not enough money in the checking account for the month, then make other arrangements (borrow, if necessary) in time so that the checking account is not overdrawn, which results in bank fees, returned check fees, and a bad credit rating.

Online Bill Paying. This method allows you to avoid writing checks or being surprised by a charge to the account that you forgot to enter on the check register. With online bill paying, you decide the amount and the time that a bill will be paid. However, since this is not automatic, you must remember to go online to pay the bill or the bill will not be paid.

Online bill paying is still easier than having to write a check, but you have the same flexibility as writing checks – you decide when and how much you will pay. This service is good for any bill that can be paid online such as credit cards, utilities, and auto loan. This method also works with any electronic bills received.

Cash. Never send cash in the mail to pay a bill. You will not have proof that the bill was paid and disputes may arise as to how much you paid. You can use cash to pay bills in person, but always get a receipt showing when and how much you paid. Keep this receipt just as you would keep the bank statement and cancelled checks (checks received with the checking account statement from the bank).

Money Orders. Until a checking account is established, you may need to pay bills using money orders. The post office, grocery stores, banks, and others issue a money order to pay a bill. However, they charge a fee for the money order and require that you pay them in cash for the amount of the money order and their fee.

Using a money order is the most inefficient and costly way to pay bills. Try to get the checking account established as soon as possible. Remember; never send cash in the mail.

NOTES

Paying Bills

Key Points

- Checks are the most common way to pay bills

- Credit cards can pay for monthly bills as well current purchases

- Automatic payments from the checking account save time

- Online bill paying saves time and you control when the payment is made

- When paying with cash, always get a receipt

- Never send cash in the mail

- Money orders are an expensive and inefficient way to pay bills

NOTES

CHAPTER SIX
Savings and Investments

As a student, you may not be in a position to start a long term savings program. But most students will need to save some of the part-time paychecks to help pay for college expenses. Even if the information in this chapter does not apply to you today, savings and investments will be important when you graduate. It is never too early to learn about saving and investing options so that when the opportunity to save presents itself, you will have an idea of the options available. If you find this topic interesting, you may wish to take a college course to further your knowledge about savings and investments.

Key players on a financial team are savings and investments accounts. You need to manage these players to be sure that they are earning the best rate of return. If not, you need to retire the current players from the team and hire new players who perform better.

For example, passbook savings accounts that you may have used since you were young may be earning 2% interest. Today, online money market accounts (which are also FDIC insured) may be earning 4% interest. By moving savings from a 2% savings account to a 4% money market account, you have doubled your earnings.

Pay Yourself First. One of the sayings that you may have heard is "to pay yourself first." In practice, this means that you should save for things that are important before monthly expenses. You may wish to save for emergencies, a vacation, car, and/or home. This guide is not intended to give financial advice, but should help you ask the right questions in deciding which investments are right for you. Outlined below are some methods used to save and some suggestions as where to place your savings.

Direct Deposit of Savings. You should always make saving easy. The best way to do this is to have savings go directly from your employer to your savings account. That way, you never have the money to spend and it will be easier to adjust your living style based on your take-home pay – net pay after taxes, benefit deductions, and savings.

Transfer Savings Each Paycheck. However, if your employer doesn't provide direct deposit into a savings account, then transfer savings when you receive your paycheck. Either write a check to the savings account or have an automatic transfer from the checking account to your savings account. This does require some effort, but is very important to have savings for really important things.

Small Purchases. Watching the small purchases will help you to save. For example, if you save just $5.00 a day by forgoing small purchases or by shopping for the best deal on everyday purchases such as gas, groceries, lunch, and meals out, you can save over $1,800 a year. Over ten years, the savings would be over $18,000! Those small purchases do matter.

Over-Withholding Income Taxes. Having too much income tax withheld from your paycheck results in an interest-free loan to the government. Receiving a tax refund is always nice, but a better way to go is to have the money in your savings account, earning interest. At the end of the year, the excess tax withholding amount would already be in your savings account, as well as interest earned on the savings during the year. As mentioned above, have your employer transfer the excess tax withholding directly to your savings account so that you have the same take home pay, but your savings account is growing with each paycheck.

Use Form W-4 to have your employer increase the federal income tax withholding allowances to reduce the federal income tax withheld. States have a similar form that can be used to reduce state income tax withheld, if your state has income taxes.

Accumulating Savings in Your Checking Account. After you have met the requirements for free checking (i.e., minimum balance requirement), move all excess funds to a savings or money market account to earn higher interest and to avoid mixing savings with the checking account, which means that you will be less likely to spend the savings on everyday purchases.

Emergency Savings. The decision about how much to save is an extremely important decision. Most financial planners suggest that emergency savings should be six months of salary. The emergency savings account should be one where you can withdraw the savings without any penalties. These accounts are usual called savings accounts or money market accounts. The key is to shop for the account that will permit immediate access to your savings, is FDIC-insured, and pays the highest interest rate. Like everything else dealing with money, shop for the savings or money market account that meets your needs.

Big Purchase Savings. The purchase of a car is expensive and may require a down payment. You will need to save for this purchase. Pay as much down as possible to reduce the monthly payments and the amount of interest on the loan (see Chapter Twelve on buying a car).

Keep these funds in a savings account or money market account. These funds can be in the same account as the emergency savings.

Retirement Savings. The furthest thing from your mind right now is retirement. Someday, when you retire, you will be entitled to social security payments and perhaps a pension payment from your employer. These sources of retirement income are generally not sufficient to support you in retirement. Therefore, try to start a retirement plan as early as possible.

The government actually encourages you to save for retirement by not taxing amounts (within certain limits) that are contributed to the retirement savings. If the retirement savings are withdrawn before age 59½, you may have to pay a 10% penalty and pay the income tax on the amount withdrawn. Two important exceptions to the 10% penalty for a withdrawal from an Individual Retirement Account (IRA) are if the withdrawal is used to pay for qualified higher education expenses or to buy your first home.

It is never too early to start saving for retirement. The earlier you start saving for retirement, the more retirement savings you will have because you will be contributing longer, as well as earning a return on the savings longer.

For example, if you start a retirement savings program at age twenty-one by saving $100 a month ($1,200 a year) until age sixty-one (40 years) and earn an average of a 5% return on the savings, the retirement fund would be $153,000. However, if you do not start the same savings program until age thirty-one, the retirement fund will only be $83,000 or $70,000 less in the retirement fund at age sixty-one. The reason there is $70,000 less in the retirement fund is because you contributed $12,000 less ($1,200 x ten years) to the fund and earned $58,000 less on the savings because you started the savings program ten years later.

Everyone understands that the earlier he or she starts a savings program, the larger the retirement amount will be. What most people don't realize is the magnitude of the difference in the retirement amount by starting a retirement savings program later in life.

Types of retirement accounts include employer retirement savings plans (401 (K)) and Individual Retirement Accounts (IRAs). These plans are outlined below.

Employer Retirement Savings Plan (401 (K)). If your employer has a retirement savings plan that includes an employer match, you should try to contribute an amount which would result in the employer contributing the maximum amount to your account.

For example, some employers will match contributions to the 401 (K) plan on a dollar for dollar basis up to 3% of salary. If you contribute 3% of your salary, the employer would also contribute 3% of your salary. Therefore, you are receiving 6% of your salary in your 401 (K) plan even though it costs you only 3% of your salary. Amounts contributed to an employer retirement savings plan are generally deductible for tax purposes.

Some of the employer matching programs don't vest for several years. Vest means that the money in the plan is yours. For example, assume that the employer savings plan requires that you work for two years before the employer match vests, but your contributions to the plan vests immediately. If you should leave before you have worked two years, then you would not receive the employer match. However, you receive all of your contributions and the related earnings when you leave, even if you leave before you have worked two years. Be sure that you understand the vesting requirements for the employer retirement savings plan.

Individual Retirement Accounts (IRAs). These accounts are set up at banks or stockbrokers, depending on whether you want to invest in cash savings (such as money markets or certificates of deposit) or invest in the stock market (individual stocks or mutual funds). Amounts contributed to these accounts are tax deductible, so you save on income taxes – just as with the employer retirement savings plan.

Unlike the employer retirement savings plans, there is no match for contributions to an IRA. Your contribution to the IRA is the only amount going into your IRA. There are limits to the amount you can contribute each year ($4,000 per person for 2007) and, at high income levels, no amount can be contributed to an IRA. Remember, contributions to an IRA are for retirement and are subject to a 10% penalty (subject to exceptions) if any of the money is withdrawn from an IRA before age 59 ½.

Where to Invest Savings. Factors to consider when deciding where to invest savings include the amount of risk involved and the time frame for the investment. Types of investments include cash (money market accounts and certificates of deposit), stocks, bonds, mutual funds, and real estate.

Short Term Savings. If saving for short term or emergency savings, consider cash savings such as money market accounts or certificates of deposit (with a short maturity date – the date when the savings can be withdrawn without paying a bank penalty). These funds should be in an account insured by the FDIC which guarantees that if the bank goes out of business, you will recover savings up to $100,000 per account. You may be promised a higher interest rate by someone who does not have FDIC insurance, but you could lose part or all of your savings. This risk may not be worth taking.

Money Market Mutual Funds. Another option to consider for short term savings is money market mutual funds offered by stockbrokers. Although money market mutual funds are not FDIC insured, they may be a safe investment if the fund holds government debt. Be sure that the stockbroker is a member of Securities Investor Protection Corporation (SIPC). The SIPC does not insure against the fund losing value (risk assumed by the investor), but does provide some protection against stockbroker theft or if the brokerage fails.

Like money market accounts at banks, money market mutual funds are very liquid which means you can take your money out of the fund on short notice. Generally, money market mutual funds pay a higher return than money market accounts because of the higher risk for a money market mutual fund (you may lose some of your investment). You must be comfortable that the additional return is worth the additional risk before placing your savings in a money market mutual fund. Otherwise, place your savings in a bank money market account insured by the FDIC.

Longer Term Savings. For retirement savings or savings for over five years, you may wish to diversify savings by investing in stocks or mutual funds through a stockbroker. The stockbroker should be a member of the Securities Investor Protection Corporation (SIPC). Just as with banks, shop to determine which stockbroker meets your needs. For example, deal with a stockbroker that has no-load mutual funds and a low commission rate on stock purchases.

Mutual Funds. If you have small amounts of money to invest, mutual funds are a good way to invest. Some mutual funds also permit diversification by investing in stocks and bonds in the same fund.

When looking for a mutual fund, make sure there are no fees to purchase the funds – called loads. These fees can be up to 5% of the investment, which means that you immediately lose 5% of the savings. Some of the funds have a back-end load, which means that if the money is moved within a period of time (say seven years), there will be a fee charged. Never, never, never invest in a fund that charges a fee either up-front or back-end. There are many no-load funds available.

Also, consider the annual expense to operate the fund. The higher the expense, the lower the return will be. Always look for a quality fund which has a low annual expense.

Stocks and Bonds. Once you have accumulated significant savings, you may decide to invest in individual stocks and bonds. This will clearly have more risk and you could lose some, if not all, of your savings. Diversification is important to minimizing risks by investing in several stocks and/or bonds.

Also, you pay commissions when stock is purchased and when stock is sold. These commissions can actually cause you to lose money, even though the stock goes up in value.

For example, you purchase 100 shares of a stock for $15 a share and a commission of $195 is paid. The stock goes to $18 a share and you decide to sell. The commission is again $195 to sell. You actually lose $90 because the commissions were $390 and the gain on the stock was only $300 (100 shares x $3). There are many low commission options from which to choose. By doing some research, you can save money by paying lower commissions to buy and sell stocks.

For most people, investing in several mutual funds (stock funds and bond funds) is the best way to save for long-term goals. Again, consider no-load funds with low annual expenses to maximize the net earnings on your savings.

Exhibit 6A provides a sample savings decision checklist.

Savings and Investments
Key Points

- Pay yourself first; save a portion of every paycheck

- Watch small purchases; saving $5 a day would result in over $18,000 in ten years

- Don't over-withhold income taxes from your paycheck

- Don't accumulate savings in a checking account

- Try to save six months of your salary in an emergency savings account

- Big purchase savings can be included in the emergency savings account

- Retirement savings

  - Start retirement savings plan as soon as possible
  - Contribute enough to receive the maximum employer match in an Employer 401 (K) plan
  - Contribute as much as possible (up to the maximum limit) each year in an IRA

- Invest savings

  - For emergency and short term, consider money market or certificates of deposit
  - For retirement, consider mutual funds that are no-load funds with low annual expenses

- Financial institutions

  - Bank should be a member of FDIC
  - Stockbroker should be a member of SIPC

NOTES

TOPAZ CONSULTING, LLC

Exhibit 6A – Decision Checklist for Savings

Page 1 of 2

- **Decide how much to save**
  - Decide on a percent of earnings or an annual amount

- **Decide where to save. Allocate your savings to the following saving plans**
  - Company retirement plans
    - Contribute enough to receive the maximum company match
    - Long term savings are not readily accessible

  - Individual Retirement Accounts (IRA)
    - Contribute the maximum permitted by law ($4,000 for 2007)
    - Long term savings are not readily accessible

  - Emergency fund
    - Save six months income in a readily accessible account

  - Long term savings
    - Set goal for car and home purchase
    - Set target date when you expect to need funds

- **Decide what investments you want to make for each savings plan**
  - Company retirement plans
    - Diversify; don't invest all of your savings in company stock
    - Select investment based on savings options offered in plan

  - Individual Retirement Accounts (IRA)
    - Diversify
      - Put cash in savings account, money market, or certificates of deposit
      - Buy mutual funds with no-load and low annual expenses
        - Stock funds, bond funds, or stock/bond funds
      - Buy individual stocks and bonds; select low commission broker

  - Emergency fund
    - Keep in cash in order to have ready access to funds in emergency
      - Maintain savings account or money market account
        - Money market accounts generally pay more interest than savings accounts

Exhibit 6A – Decision Checklist for Savings

- Long term savings
    - Depends on when you need the funds
        - Generally, do not put funds in mutual funds, stocks, or bonds, if you will need the funds within five years
    - Savings account probably doesn't pay high enough interest
    - Money market account yields higher interest than savings account
    - Certificates of deposit (CD)
        - CDs may pay higher interest rates, but there is a penalty if you cash the CD before maturity
        - CDs should mature on or before the date you plan to use the funds
        - Create a CD ladder so that CDs have different maturity dates
    - Mutual funds and stocks
        - Look for no-load mutual funds with low annual expenses
        - Stock funds offer diversification with stocks
        - Bond funds offer diversification with bonds
        - Stock/bond funds offer both stock and bond diversification
        - Index funds offer maximum diversification by investing in an entire market

- **Decide on financial institution**
    - Banks
        - Should be member of FDIC
        - Pay the highest rate on the type of savings you plan to have
            - One bank may pay a higher interest rate on money markets and another bank may pay a higher rate for certificates of deposit
        - Should provide online accessibility to accounts
        - You can have more than one bank to invest your savings

    - Stockbrokers
        - Should be member of SIPC
        - Should offer no-load mutual funds with low annual expenses
        - Should offer low commission rates on stock trades
        - Should provide online accessibility to accounts
        - You perhaps should have only one stockbroker

TOPAZ CONSULTING, LLC

NOTES

CHAPTER SEVEN
Financial Applications

Anytime you open a checking account, savings account, investment account, borrow money, or purchase insurance, you will be required to provide information about your personal and financial situation. As you complete this guide, most of the information you will need to complete these applications will be available as part of your financial record-keeping system.

Application Instructions. Most applications will provide instructions on how to complete the application. It is important that you understand what information is required and you supply that information as accurately as possible. Never intentionally make a false statement on any application that you complete. False statements can lead to serious consequences, including termination of insurance or default on the loan (which means that the entire loan balance will be currently due).

Application Considerations. Before you complete and sign a financial application, be sure that you understand the terms to which you are agreeing. For example, the terms for a checking account may include no monthly fee if a minimum balance is maintained. For a loan, the interest rate and the monthly payment amount are extremely important. For an insurance policy, the coverage limits and the premium amount are key terms.

Review all applications before you sign them to be sure that they are completed accurately. Also, verify that the terms and conditions in the application are the same as those presented in any promotional material.

Be sure to keep a copy of all applications that you sign and keep a copy of all materials, especially information about the terms. These documents will be very helpful if a dispute should develop in the future.

Signing the Application. Don't take the signing of a financial application lightly. When you sign an application you are confirming that all information on the application is correct. If the information is not correct, you could be held liable for making a false statement.

You are also authorizing the company to verify information about you including your employment and your credit history. The company has your permission to contact your employer as well as to contact the credit bureaus about your credit report. This inquiry into your credit could have a negative effect on your credit score, if you have a lot of credit inquires. Chapter Fourteen on managing your credit has more information about credit reports.

In addition, you are agreeing to the terms of the application, even if you do not understand the terms. Therefore, you need to take the time to fully understand the terms of the application. For example, the interest rate on a store credit card may be zero percent for twelve months and then goes to 24% after twelve months. If this is the case, you need to pay the entire balance before the interest rate goes to 24%. If do not have the money, borrow money from another source at a lower interest to pay off this balance.

Financial Information. The financial information required on the application will generally include your income and expenses (this information is available from your budget – Chapter Sixteen) and your assets and liabilities (this information is available from your net worth statement – Chapter Seventeen).

Remember, when you sign the application, you are giving the lender permission to contact your employer to verify your salary and to request a credit report from the credit bureaus to verify your credit rating and your liabilities. Therefore, you may wish to request your free credit report from the credit bureaus before applying for a loan. Chapter Fourteen explains how to request your free credit report and describes the type of information that is in your credit report.

Checking, Savings, and Investment Accounts. When you open a checking, savings, or investment account, you will be required to open the account in person and to present identification that you are who you say you are. All persons on the account must be present to open an account. Forms of identification include driver's license, passport, and social security card. If you have to use your social security card as identification, return your social security card to a safe place as soon as possible and do not routinely carry your social security card in your wallet or purse.

You should call the financial institution to determine what types of identification are acceptable to open an account with them. This could save you from having to make a second trip to present the proper identification required to open the account.

Credit Card Application. Generally, a credit card application, including a store credit card application, will describe the terms of the credit card. The interest rate (select a credit card with the lowest interest rate available), the annual fee (should be zero or apply for a different credit card), and other charges such as late payment fees and over credit limit charges are generally summarized in the application.

If the terms of the credit card are not presented to you, request this information before you sign the application. Be sure that you understand the terms of the credit card and always keep a copy of any credit card application that you sign along with the terms of the credit card.

You will probably receive dozens of credit card applications in the mail. Review the terms of the card and determine if the terms are better than the terms on your current credit card. If so, you may wish to change credit cards. Be sure that the application is real and is not a scam to get your personal information. Also note that the credit card company will contact the credit bureau for a credit report and this can cause your credit score to drop if there are excessive inquiries into your credit history.

Generally, you will be better served to shop for a good credit card and keep that card which will help your credit history as explained in Chapter Fourteen. You should have no more than two credit cards at a time.

Loan Application. Types of loans include auto loan, personal loan, education loans, and home loan (mortgage or equity line of credit). Most loan applications will require that you provide information regarding your income (to be sure that you can repay the loan) and your net worth – your assets and liabilities (to be sure that the lender can collect the debt from your net assets if you don't pay as promised).

Be sure you understand the terms of the loan – the interest rate, the monthly payment, fees required, late payment charges, and any prepayment penalties (you should not have a loan with a prepayment penalty). The terms of the loan will probably permit the lender to sell your assets to pay the loan if you do not make your payments as promised.

For example, if you do not make your car payments on time, the lender could sell your car and use the money from the sale of the car to pay the auto loan. If the car sale does not provide enough money to pay the auto loan in full, then the lender could sell some of your other assets to satisfy the remaining balance. Therefore, it is extremely important that you are sure that you can make the monthly payments from your income on any loan.

After you are comfortable with the information on the loan application and you understand the terms of the loan, you can then sign the application. Keep a copy of the signed application, a summary of the terms of the loan, and any other information pertaining to the loan.

Insurance Application. When you apply for insurance (auto, home, health, life, and disability), you will be required to complete the insurance company's application for insurance.

It is extremely important that all information you provide on the insurance application is accurate. If not, your insurance may be cancelled and you could receive no insurance benefits because the insurance company could argue that it would not have provided the insurance if it had known the correct facts. Typically, this false information will come to light when you file an insurance claim which is absolutely the worse time to have your insurance cancelled.

NOTES

Financial Applications
Key Points

- The application instructions

  - Never intentionally make a false statement

- For all applications

  - Understand the terms before you sign
  - Complete all information before you sign
  - Keep a copy of all signed applications and any information pertaining to the terms

- By signing the application, you

  - Confirm that all information is correct
  - Authorize the company to verify the information
  - Agree to the terms of application

- Financial information required

  - Income and expenses (budget)
  - Assets and liabilities (net worth statement)

- Checking, savings, and investment accounts

  - Open in person
  - Present identification documents

- Credit card application

    - Don't apply for every credit card offer received
    - Company will check your credit report
    - Two credit cards should be sufficient

- Loan application

    - Be sure that you can pay as promised
    - Company will check your credit report

- Insurance application

    - Complete as accurately as possible
    - Company may check your credit report

CHAPTER EIGHT
Scholarships, Grants, and Student Loans

The cost of a college education continues to increase each year making it difficult to "afford" to go to college. Most people have not been able to save enough money to send their children to college. Therefore, students have to look for sources of money to finance their college education. The chapter will outline some of the sources available to assist with your college expenses.

Types of Financial Aid. Scholarships and grants are the best type of money for college expenses because the amounts received do not need to be repaid. This money is truly free and you should try to obtain as much money in scholarships and grants as possible.

Federal work-study programs also provide money for college. These are campus-based programs that provide jobs for students with financial needs.

To pay for any remaining college expenses, you may need to apply for a student loan, either a federally guaranteed loan or a private loan. The interest charged on these loans and the principal borrowed must be repaid in accordance with the terms of the loan.

Strategies for Funding College Expenses. First, you should investigate scholarships and grants. Scholarships and grants are based on need and/or merit. Therefore, you may qualify for assistance even if your family income exceeds the level that qualifies for assistance based on need. Contact your college financial aid office and search the Internet for scholarships. Also, investigate company (where you or your parents work) and community (where you went to high school) scholarships. Be sure that all scholarship offers are legitimate. You do not have to pay to find scholarships.

As explained below, complete the Free Application for Federal Student Aid (FAFSA) form as soon as possible after January 1. Based on the FAFSA information, you will receive a Student Aid Report (SAR) and your college will receive a report from the Department of Education. Your college will use this report to send you a financial aid package which indicates the amounts and kinds of financial aid (federal, state, and college) available to you.

Select your financial aid in the order that will cost you the least amount. For example, select scholarships and grants first, then select loans (subsidized federal loans) that defer interest until you have completed college, and then select loans (unsubsidized federal and private loans) with the lowest interest rates. Remember, scholarships and grants do not have to be repaid, but the principal (amount borrowed) and interest on all types of loans must be repaid in accordance with the terms of the loans.

Federal Financial Aid. Depending on your income, federal financial aid for education may be the first place to start your search for college money. The federal government provides scholarships, grants, work-study programs, and federally guaranteed loans.

To qualify for any of these federal programs, you must complete the Free Application for Federal Student Aid (FAFSA) form. The FAFSA form should be completed as soon after January 1 as possible because most funds are distributed on a first-come, first-served basis. The FAFSA form is available online at www.fafsa.ed.gov. The FAFSA form must be re-submitted for each year you're enrolled in college. Be sure to read the instructions carefully and to keep a copy of the completed FAFSA form for your records.

Federal Grants. The Pell Grant and the Federal Supplemental Education Opportunity Grant (FSEOG) are two federal grants that are need-based and are available to students with annual family income below $35,000. The awards are from $400 to $4,050 for the Pell Grant and from $100 to $4,000 for the FSEOG. As mentioned above, grants do not have to be repaid.

If you are eligible to receive a Pell Grant, you may qualify for the Academic Competitiveness Grant or the National SMART Grant. Both of these grants are new for the 2006-2007 school year and are in addition to your Pell Grant award.

The Academic Competitiveness Grant will provide up to $750 for first year undergraduate students and up to $1,300 for second year undergraduate students. To qualify for this grant you must have completed a rigorous high school program. Second year students must have also maintained a 3.0 cumulative grade point average.

The National SMART Grant will provide up to $4,000 for each of the third and fourth years of undergraduate study for students majoring in physical science, life science, computer science, mathematics, technology, engineering, or critical foreign language. You must maintain a cumulative grade point average of at least a 3.0 in the coursework required for the major.

Federal Student Loans. If your scholarships, grants, savings and parent's payments are not enough money to pay for your college expenses, you should consider federal student loans. These loans typically provide lower interest rates than commercial interest rates and defer repayment of the loan until after you leave college. Therefore, you do not make payments on your federal student loan while you are in college, but you must repay this loan just like any other loan after college. Remember, the more you borrow, the more principal and interest you have to repay. Therefore, you should minimize the amount of money you borrow from any source, including federal student loans.

You need to understand your repayment obligation under a federal student loan or any loan. If you don't repay your student loan on time, you could be in default of your legal obligation which has serious consequences and will adversely affect your credit score. The types of federal student loans are the Stafford loan and the Perkins loan which are described below.

Stafford Loan. One of the federal education loans available to students is the Stafford loan which can be subsidized (the loan does not accrue interest while the student is in school) or unsubsidized (interest begins to accrue immediately). Stafford loans are not based on financial need. The repayment of this loan begins six months after graduation or after the student ceases to be enrolled in school at least half-time. The fixed interest rate for loans after July 1, 2006 is 6.8%.

The maximum amount that can be borrowed using a Stafford loan is $2,625 for the first year, $3,500 for the second year, $5,500 for the third year, and $5,500 for the fourth year of college for a dependent student (a student who relies on his or her parents for support). A student who is not dependent on his or her parents for support (independent student) can borrow $6,625 in the first year, $7,500 in the second year, $10,500 in the third year, and $10,500 in the fourth year of college. The maximum amount that can be subsidized (interest not accruing while the student is in college) for both the dependent and the independent student is $23,000.

Perkins Loan. Another federal education loan available to students is the Perkins loan which is a low-interest (five percent) loan for both undergraduate and graduate students with exceptional financial need. The maximum amount that can be borrowed is $4,000 per year for undergraduates.

The amount you can borrow will depend on when you apply, your financial need, and the funding level at the college you are attending. Payments on the loan will start nine months after you graduate, leave school, or drop below half-time status.

PLUS Loan (Parent Loan for Undergraduate Students). Parents can borrow using a PLUS loan to help pay education expenses if the student is a dependent undergraduate student. The PLUS loan is a federal education loan that is available either through the college (Direct PLUS loan) or through a lender (Federal Family Education Loan or FFEL PLUS loan). The parents must have acceptable credit history in order to qualify for a PLUS loan. Although a FAFSA form is not required for a PLUS loan, dependent students should complete the FAFSA form to ensure that they receive the maximum student financial aid available.

The maximum amount that can be borrowed using a PLUS Loan is equal to your cost of attending college minus any other financial aid you receive (grants, federal work study, other federal loans, etc.). The current interest rate is fixed at 7.94% for a Direct PLUS Loan and 8.5% for a FFEL PLUS Loan. Your parents may have to pay a fee of up to 4% of the loan which will be deducted from the proceeds of the loan.

The money from a PLUS Loan is paid directly to your college. Repayment of the PLUS Loan begins 60 days after the money has been disbursed. Therefore, your parents must begin repaying both the principal and interest while you are in college.

Repayment Plans. Some of the repayment plans available for federal student loans are standard (fixed monthly amount with up to 10 years to repay), extended (from 12 to 30 years to repay), graduated (payments increase over time and you have from 12 to 30 years to repay), and income contingent (payments are based on your adjusted gross income, family size, interest rate, and loan amount).

Another good feature of a federal student loan is that you can repay the loan early without a prepayment penalty. Also, there are provisions that permit you to consolidate your federal student loans after graduation in order to simplify your loan repayment.

Your student loan account balance and status is regularly reported to the national credit bureaus. Therefore, repaying your student loan on time will increase your credit score.

Default. If you don't make your monthly payments as promised in the repayment plan, you will be in default on the loan which results in serious consequences. If default occurs, some of the consequences include (i) the entire loan balance (principal and interest) will be immediately due, (ii) your account could be turned over to a collection agency (you will owe additional collection costs), (iii) the national credit bureaus will be notified of the default (your credit rating will be damaged), and (iv) your employer may be required to withhold (garnish) part of your salary to repay the loan.

Treat a student loan like any other financial obligation. Be sure that you understand the terms of your loan. You must be able to repay the loan as promised or serious financial consequences will occur as outlined above.

Non-Federal Loans. You can borrow money from any source to pay for your college expenses, but the federal loans mentioned above may provide you with better terms (interest rate, fees, and repayment schedule). Other sources of loans include family, friends, banks, and credit unions. Remember, these are loans and must be repaid in accordance with their terms.

More Information. You should treat the above information as a summary of some of the programs available to assist you in funding your college education. There may be more options available at the college you attend and you should contact your college's financial aid office for guidance.

The Department of Education Federal Student Aid website at www.studentaid.ed.gov provides additional information regarding the federal student aid programs.

NOTES

Scholarships and Student Loans

Key Points

- Types of student financial aid

    - Scholarships – don't have to repay
    - Grants – don't have to repay
    - Work study – must work (no repayment)
    - Loans – must be repaid, including interest

- Federal student financial aid

    - Complete FAFSA form
    - Federal grants – Pell, FSEOG, Academic, SMART
    - Work study
    - Student loans – Stafford and Perkins
    - Parent loan – PLUS

- Federal student loan repayment plans

    - Standard
    - Extended
    - Graduated
    - Income contingent

- Default on federal student loan

    - Entire balance due immediately
    - Incur collection agency fees
    - Reduce credit score
    - Garnish of salary to repay loan

- Private loans

    - May be more expensive than federal student loans
    - Repayment plans may not be as flexible as federal student loans

- Additional information contact

    - College financial aid office
    - U.S. Department of Education

CHAPTER NINE
Credit Card Use

If used properly, credit cards are a great financial tool for students. But they can also cause financial disaster because of the high interest rate, potential expensive fees, and identity theft. In addition, credit cards allow you to overspend because the credit card limit may be higher than the amount you can afford to spend each month. This is especially true if you have more than one credit card.

Selecting a Credit Card. Shop for a credit card just as you would shop for anything else. There are many credit card providers and their terms vary greatly. First, the credit card should not have an annual fee. Second, look for a credit card provider with a low interest rate on unpaid balances; some rates are as low as 8%. You certainly do not want a credit card that charges over 20% interest on unpaid balances. Third, look for a credit card that gives you a refund on purchases made using the card – up to a 3% refund.

Best Use of a Credit Card. Clearly, you should only use a credit card to make a purchase that you can afford. Rather than use cash or a check, you can use a credit card to make the purchase. But, you should have the cash in the bank or savings account to pay for the purchase.

You can have some monthly bills paid automatically with your credit card. For example, rather than paying a utility bill by check or by debiting your checking account, you can have the utility charge your credit card for the monthly bill. The money will stay in your checking account longer. Also, your checking account will be easier to reconcile because you will not have written a check or have a debit to your checking account that you have to enter in your check register. You should not pay a service fee to use a credit card to pay a monthly bill. If a fee is required, then you should use another method to pay the bill.

To monitor your credit card balance, you should retain copies of all credit card receipts and each week add up the credit card receipts and any automatic payments to the credit card to determine the amount you owe on the credit card.

If you have online banking, you can review your credit card balances at any time. But again, review the online credit card account at least weekly to determine your balance. Be cautious about the online balance because it may take several days for a purchase to be posted to the credit card account.

As part of your budgeting process, determine how much you can spend using your credit card each month, including automatic payments suggested above. Once you reach your limit, you should stop spending. Chapter Sixteen provides more information on budgeting.

Since each credit card requires monitoring and payments each month, the fewer credit cards you have, the easier it will be for you to manage these cards. Two credit cards should be the maximum number to have.

Be sure to pay the entire credit card balance each month before the due date and enjoy the free use of someone else's money.

Credit Card Issues. As long as you stay on top of credit card balances and make payments in full each billing cycle by the due date, the credit card will produce positive benefits. But if you neglect your credit card and permit the balances to get out of control, you can be in big financial trouble.

Interest rates on unpaid credit balances can be over 20% for many credit cards. Credit card fees for late payments and over credit limit charges are expensive. Some credit cards actually start the interest on the day you purchase an item if the previous credit card statement balance is not paid in full before the due date.

If you don't make at least the minimum credit card payments on time, your credit score will plummet (which is not a good thing). Likewise, if the credit card balance exceeds 50% of your credit limit, you will take another hit to your credit score. A low credit score is very bad for your financial health (as explained in Chapter Fourteen).

Of course, if your credit card is stolen, you must report the theft and go through all the steps to correct any unauthorized charges to your account (as explained in Chapter Fifteen on identity theft).

One of the major reasons people get into financial trouble is because they have several credit cards which they use to make purchases. The credit limits on all the cards exceed the person's ability to pay the balance due each month. You must monitor your purchases to know that the amount you have spent is within your budget. Do not rely on the credit card credit limit to stop you from spending.

Credit Card Benefits. Credit cards eliminate the need to write checks (which are becoming more difficult to cash) and to carry large sums of cash to make everyday purchases. You do not have to pay for items purchased with credit cards until the due date of the credit card which may be several weeks after the purchase. This gives you free use of money until the due date of the credit card, but only if you pay the credit card balance in full each month.

Using a credit card will also allow you to build a credit history and can increase your credit score if you make payments on time and the outstanding balance on the credit card is under 50% of the credit limit on the credit card.

Using Credit Cards for Loans. Credit cards charge notoriously high interest rates. Therefore, use credit cards to borrow money only as a last resort. If you must borrow using a credit card, then select a credit card that has the lowest possible interest rate. Credit card interest rates can range from 8% to over 20%.

Store Credit Cards. A word about store credit cards is appropriate because they have the same issues as the national credit cards. However, these cards can only be used at the store which issued the card. You need to understand the terms for using the store credit cards. The interest rates for store credit cards may be much higher than the national credit cards.

If a store credit card offers a low interest rate, be sure to understand the terms. For example, maybe the interest rate is zero for one year; you can't beat a zero interest rate. But, this rate may be contingent upon your making monthly payments and, if you don't, the interest rate could go from 0% to 24%. Or perhaps, the interest rate is good for one year, and then the rate goes to 24%. If so, be sure you pay the balance in full by the end of the year to avoid this high interest rate.

Credit Card Disputes. If you disagree with a credit card charge, you must follow the dispute procedures of your credit card agreement to protect yourself from unauthorized charges. Generally, these procedures require you to notify, in writing, the credit card company about a disputed charge within a specified period of time after the disputed charge is posted to your credit card.

Credit Card Use
Key Points

- Credit card selection

  - No annual fee
  - Low interest rate
  - Refund on purchases

- Best use of a credit card

  - Only purchase items that you can afford
  - Use instead of cash or a check
  - Pay routine monthly bills
  - Monitor balance every week
  - Pay the entire balance each month before the due date

- Credit card issues

  - High interest rates if balance is not paid in full each month
  - Negative effect on credit score if minimum payment is not made
  - Negative effect on credit score if you have excess balance
  - If card is stolen, you may have identity theft issues
  - Ease of overspending

- Benefits of credit card

  - Eliminates need for cash or checks for purchases
  - Free use of money, if balance is paid each month
  - Creates credit history which could increase credit score
  - Increases credit score if the balance is under 50% of credit limit

- Credit card loans

  - High interest rates
  - Last resort to borrow

- Store credit cards

  - Same issues as national credit cards
  - Probably higher interest rates than national credit cards

- Credit card disputes

  - Must be in writing
  - Must be within time period allowed

CHAPTER TEN
Debt Management

As a student, you may need to borrow to provide money to pay for your college expenses. Chapter Eight explains student loans in detail. This chapter reviews other types of loans that you may need during your lifetime.

Borrowing money can be compared to golf: the lower the score (interest rate), the better. You need to have players on your team that can deliver low interest rates.

For example, credit cards are a great financial tool to use to make purchases, but they charge notoriously high interest rates. Therefore, borrow money using credit cards only as a last resort. If you do not pay credit card balances in full each month to avoid interest charges, then select a credit card that has the lowest possible interest rate. Credit card interest rates can range from 8% to over 20%.

Debt management is extremely important to your financial health. If you fail to make loan payments on time, your credit score will fall, which means that the next time you need to borrow, you will pay a higher interest rate. If you miss enough loan payments, you might not be able to borrow the next time you need a loan. Further, the loan company has the right to sell your property if you fail to make payments on time. If this happens, you will lose equity in the property; that is, the property may sell for less than it is worth.

Paying loans on time is extremely important. If you do not make payments on time, (i) you will pay late payment charges on the current loan; (ii) you may be denied a loan in the future; (iii) you may pay a higher interest rate on future loans; (iv) property could be sold at a price that is less than the real value in order to repay the loan; and (v) your credit score will be reduced.

To avoid the disaster of not being able to repay loans as promised, be careful where and how much you borrow. Manage your money so that you can repay any loan as promised. As explained in Chapter Sixteen, a budget is a great tool to assist you with debt management.

Costs of Loans. When you borrow money, there are always costs involved. First, there may be up-front fees, such as loan processing fees. Second, there is always an interest rate, which may be zero for a short period of time. Third, there will be late payment fees if payments are not made on time. And finally, there may be early payment charges – if the loan is repaid early. Your goal should be to minimize all four types of loan costs.

Types of Loans. Loans are available from many sources and you must take care to choose the type of loan that meets your needs. First, loans from family and friends are a source of money when you are starting out. Second, credit cards provide a source of borrowing by letting you purchase things with the card and then pay later, but interest rates are usually very high (See Chapter Nine on credit card use). As a student, you will probably need a student loan. Most people need an auto loan to purchase a car. Likewise, when you purchase a home, you most likely will need a home mortgage, a loan on the home being purchased. Once you own a home, then you may be able to use a home equity loan to borrow money.

Family and Friends. There is an old saying that the quickest way to lose a friend is to loan him or her money. Nevertheless, family and friends can be a source of money when you are just starting out. But, be absolutely sure that you can repay this loan as promised. If you don't, you will probably lose their friendship forever over money. They will not loan you the money if they do not care about you and believe that you will repay them. So take this type of loan very, very seriously.

Credit Cards. Unfortunately, too many people use credit cards to borrow money. With interest rates over 20%, this can be a financial disaster and can cause people to go into bankruptcy. Never borrow money using a credit card with an interest rate over 20%. Credit cards are a good financial resource to use, but you will be well served to pay credit cards in full each month in order to avoid the high interest rate.

Store Credit Cards. These cards can only be used at the store which issued the card. Be sure that the terms for using the store credit cards are understood. Their interest rates may be much higher than the national credit cards.

Student Loans. With the high cost of college education, most students will need to borrow to pay for their college education. Student loans are described in Chapter Eight.

Auto Loans. Most people need to borrow when they buy a car. The car dealer will most likely offer to arrange for the auto loan needed to buy the auto. Again, like everything else, shop the auto loan. You just made a good deal on the car; now make a good deal on the auto loan. The dealer's loan offer is certainly a good place to start shopping for an auto loan.

Compare the total cost of the loan: (i) up-front costs such as processing fees; (ii) the interest rate – which should be computed using simple interest and not what is called the Rule of 78's (see below); (iii) late payment penalties; and (iv) early payment charges.

Be careful when deciding on the length of time for the auto loan. A longer term auto loan (up to six years) will result in a lower auto loan payment. However, if the auto is sold or traded after two or three years, the auto loan balance may be higher than the value of the auto. Therefore, you may have to use savings or borrow to pay off the auto loan.

Rule of 78's. The Rule of 78's is used by some lenders to calculate interest on loans. Although this method is not considered an early payment penalty, this method results in a penalty if you pay off the loan early.

For example, you purchase a used car with a three-year auto loan. At the end of the three years, you have paid the same amount of interest using either the simple interest method or the Rule of 78's method. However, if you trade the car after one year, you will have paid 55.0% of the total interest using the Rule of 78's method and 52.5% of the total interest using the simple interest method to compute interest. This results in a 2.5% early payment penalty using the Rule of 78's method. Always try to negotiate a loan using simple interest rather than the Rule of 78's method.

Home Loans (Mortgages). Your largest loan will probably be a mortgage on your home. Typically, you need to pay 20% of the purchase price and borrow 80% of the purchase price. Shopping for the best mortgage can save a lot of money. The key elements of a mortgage are the interest rate, how long you have to pay back the loan (the term), fees involved with the loan, the closing costs, and whether you need to pay an up-front percentage of the loan (called points).

The two types of mortgages are the fixed rate mortgage (interest rate remains the same for the term of the mortgage) and the adjustable rate mortgage (ARM) where the interest rate can go up during the term of the mortgage. Generally, you should not pay points which are a percent of the mortgage paid to lower the interest rate (discount points) or to pay loan costs (origination points).

For example, perhaps the payment of two points (2% of the mortgage amount) would reduce the interest rate by ¼%. These points would cost $1,600 on an $80,000 mortgage. It would take eight years to recover these points by the reduced interest paid. Chances are pretty good that you will either sell the home or refinance the mortgage in less than eight years; therefore, you would lose financially by paying the two discount points. Also, you must pay $1,600 at the home closing rather than paying the additional interest over the next eight years. Since most people struggle to come up with the other closing costs, it makes sense to skip this up-front cost.

Likewise, origination points (loan costs paid to the lender) may be more expensive than the typical lender fee. For example, a 1% origination point would be $800 on an $80,000 mortgage, but another lender may only charge a lender's fee of $350. Therefore, the 1% origination point would cost $450 more than the other lender's fee.

Home Equity Line of Credit. After you have purchased a home, you may qualify for a home equity line of credit. This loan is a second mortgage on the home and provides great flexibility in borrowing money when there is a need to borrow. Many lenders will provide this loan without any closing costs. The loan will be for a maximum amount – say $50,000.

No payments are required and no interest is due until you borrow on the home equity line of credit. The interest rates on the home equity line of credit are usually lower than the interest rates on credit card debt and may be lower than the interest rates on a car loan.

Another plus to this type of loan is that the interest may be deductible for income tax purposes; interest on a credit card or car loan is not deductible for income tax purposes. Another feature is that you can repay the loan at any time without incurring a prepayment penalty. However, minimum monthly payments are required until the loan is completely repaid. Only borrow when there is a real need for money and you know that you can pay back the loan in accordance with the terms of the loan (i.e., you will be able to make the required minimum monthly payments).

Remember, this loan is a loan on your home and if you do not make the required payments on time, the lender can sell the home to pay off this loan. In addition, you will have to pay the first mortgage loan when you sell the home.

Shop around to get the best interest rate and perhaps no closing costs on a home equity line of credit. Make sure that you understand the terms of the loan – such as minimum payments, how long the loan is good for (usually ten years), and any costs associated with the loan.

The main benefits of a home equity line of credit are that (i) it is flexible (you can borrow up to the maximum amount when there is a need for money); (ii) you can repay the loan at any time without any prepayment penalties; (iii) the interest rate is usually lower than other types of loans; and (iv) the interest paid may be deductible for tax purposes.

Debt Management
Key Points

- Make loan payments on time; if not, you

    - Incur additional costs
    - Pay higher interest rates on future loans
    - May be forced to sell property to repay the loan
    - May be denied a loan in the future
    - Damage your credit rating

- Be sure to repay loans from family and friends

- Credit cards

    - Use no-fee credit cards
    - Shop for the lowest interest rate
    - Pay in full each month to avoid interest charges

- If you use store credit cards, pay the balance in full before you have to pay a high interest rate

- Shop for the best rate using simple interest calculations for auto loans

- If you use the Rule of 78's to calculate interest, the loan will be more expensive than a simple interest loan if the loan is repaid early

- Shop for best interest rate, lowest lender fees, and closing costs for home mortgage

- Consider using home equity line of credit (if you own a home)

  - Shop for best interest rate (perhaps no closing costs)
  - Usually, interest rates are lower than auto loans and credit cards
  - Interest payments may be deductible for tax purposes
  - If not paid on time, your home can be sold to repay the loan

CHAPTER ELEVEN

Insurance

As a student, you probably only need health, auto (if you have a car), and renter's (if you live in a dorm or apartment) insurance, although a small amount of life insurance is good to have to pay for final medical and funeral expenses. Nevertheless, learning about the types of insurance will assist you in meeting your insurance needs in the future. Believe it or not, you will probably receive insurance proposals while you are a student and this guide will help you evaluate the insurance proposal.

You have been playing a good offensive financial game by earning a high interest rate on savings, negotiating great loans, paying bills on time, and increasing your credit score. Now, you should focus on putting together a defensive team to protect your assets by having the proper type and amount of insurance.

Most people don't want to think about the bad things that could happen. Nevertheless, you do need to have the proper insurance to protect your health and possessions.

Shop around for the best deal on the insurance that you decide to buy and don't settle for the first proposal you receive. All insurance proposals should be in writing so that there is no misunderstanding about the coverage (what is covered and the amount of that coverage) and the costs (called insurance premiums). Comparing the different proposals is easier if all of the details are in writing. Further, you can compare the proposals at your convenience and you do not have to rely on your memory of what the insurance agent said.

Types of Insurance. The basic types of insurance are (i) health insurance which provides payments for doctors (perhaps dentists if a dental plan is included), hospitals, and medicines; (ii) life insurance which provides cash upon death and perhaps a cash value while you are living; (iii) disability insurance which provides cash if you are unable to work because of an injury or illness; (iv) car insurance which pays to repair your car as result of an accident, pays to repair other cars in an accident if you are at fault, and pays other people for damages if you are at fault; (v) homeowner's or renter's insurance which pays to repair your home and replace your damaged or stolen property; and (vi) personal umbrella liability insurance which pays people who sue because you caused their injury.

Generally, health (including dental) insurance, life insurance, and disability insurance are offered at work. Make sure that you take advantage of any employer-provided insurance even if you have to pay a portion of the premium. Generally, you should purchase car insurance, homeowner's (or renter's) insurance, and personal umbrella liability insurance from the same insurance company which should result in savings on your total insurance bill by having one insurance company write all three insurance policies (a volume discount). Exhibit 11A provides a comparison of insurance types.

Health Insurance. In order to enjoy life, you must maintain good health and be able to afford to pay the cost of treating a major sickness or injury. Health insurance is important because most people cannot afford to pay for the treatments associated with a major illness or injury. The cost of health insurance is determined based on your current health, age, habits (if you smoke, your cost will usually be higher), and level of coverage (how much are you willing to pay).

As a student, you may be covered by your parents' health insurance plan. However, if you are not on your parents' health plan, you may be able to purchase an inexpensive health plan through your college.

If you are working, you may be able to enroll in your employer's health insurance plan which will probably be the least expensive way to buy health insurance. If your employer does not provide health insurance, ask the other employees at work what they do for health insurance. Then shop health insurance companies to get the best price.

Health insurance premiums are expensive, but there are ways to reduce the costs of health insurance. You can reduce health insurance premiums by selecting higher deductibles (the amount you agree to pay before the insurance company pays anything) and co-payments (the amount you pay for each service; for example, you may be required to pay $20 for each doctor's office visit and the insurance company pays the balance of the cost for the doctor's office visit).

Perhaps you could afford to pay $1,000 a year in medical costs, but could not manage a $25,000 medical bill. Therefore, you may decide to select a $1,000 deductible amount rather than a $250 deductible amount in order to reduce the health insurance premiums.

Another reason to have health insurance is that insurance companies negotiate lower charges for doctors, hospitals, and medicines. Therefore, even if you don't spend enough to cover the deductible, you will probably still save money by paying less for medical services by having the insurance company's discounts.

The keys to health insurance are (i) join the employer's health plan; (ii) if the employer does not have a health plan, shop for health insurance; (iii) increase the deductibles and co-payments to reduce the health insurance premium to an amount you can afford; and (iv) having health insurance will probably reduce the medical expenses because the insurance companies negotiate discounts which are passed on to you as a policyholder. You should have health insurance that at least covers a major illness or injury.

Life Insurance. As a student, you should consider life insurance to provide the necessary money to pay final medical and funeral expenses, as well as help to meet financial obligations, such as student loans, auto payments, and any other debts.

No one likes to think about dying. But death is certain; we just don't know when. Life insurance pays the policy amount upon a person's death to persons listed in the policy as beneficiaries. There are two main types of life insurance – term life insurance and whole life insurance.

Term Life Insurance. Term life insurance pays the face amount of the policy at death. If you stop paying the premiums, you terminate the term life insurance and the beneficiaries receive nothing upon death. The cost of term life insurance is generally lower than whole life insurance and is generally lower the younger you are. As people grow older, the premiums increase because it is more likely that they would die during the insurance policy term.

For example, a twenty-one year old is less likely to die within the next year than a person who is ninety years old. To insure the twenty-one year old for one year costs much less than to insure the ninety-year old for one year. Therefore, over time, the cost of term life insurance will increase. Consequently, you use term life insurance generally for short periods of time when you are young to provide the coverage you need. For example, a term life insurance policy would be beneficial when you have young children to support. After the children are grown, you no longer need this life insurance and can cancel this policy.

Whole Life Insurance. Whole life insurance also pays the face amount of the policy to beneficiaries at death. However, the insurance premiums for whole life insurance do not increase as you grow older and the insurance policy will have a value (called a cash surrender value) if you decide to cash in the policy before death. A term life insurance policy has no cash surrender value. Whole life insurance is generally considered to be permanent insurance – insurance you will keep throughout your life.

The younger you are when you purchase whole life insurance, the cheaper the premiums are to purchase the policy. Remember that the premiums do not increase after you purchase the policy; therefore, the younger you are, the lower the premiums will be for your entire life (or until you decide to stop making premium payments).

Cash surrender value grows each year as you make your insurance premium payments. You can borrow the cash surrender value if needed. However, you probably should not borrow from the insurance policy because the death benefit will be reduced by the amount of the loan. You will have to repay the loan amount and pay interest on the loan. The whole life insurance amount should be the amount that you expect to keep to pay final medical and funeral expenses; the term life insurance amount is the amount you need to cover shorter term responsibilities and you expect to drop term life insurance in the future.

In purchasing whole life insurance, consider using a mutual life insurance company rather than a stock life insurance company. If you have a policy with a mutual life insurance company, you are part owner and will receive the benefit of any profits earned by the mutual life insurance company (there are no shareholders). In a stock life insurance company, any profits go to the shareholders of the stock life insurance company and not to you as a policyholder.

The key to life insurance is to have enough insurance to provide for your loved ones in case of your death. At a minimum, each person needs enough life insurance for the final medical expenses and funeral expenses (this probably should be whole life insurance; you will keep this insurance for a lifetime).

Disability Insurance. The purpose of disability insurance is to replace part of the salary you were earning while working. If you become unable to work as result of injury or illness, disability insurance provides cash to help pay bills. Disability insurance generally covers a part of your salary if you become disabled while you are employed or while you are trying to find a job after being laid off.

Your employer may provide this insurance for a small cost. If your employer does not provide disability insurance, you can purchase this coverage on your own. The insurance premiums depend on the amount of coverage selected, which is the amount of the monthly payments you would receive while you are unable to work.

Auto Insurance. As a full time student, your car may be covered by your parents' auto insurance policy. If your parents' policy does not cover your car, you must purchase either auto insurance or uninsured motorist insurance. Generally, the only time you would purchase uninsured motorist insurance is if you do not qualify for auto insurance because of excessive traffic tickets or accidents. Auto insurance is preferable to the uninsured motorist insurance because the protection from damage and liability claims is much better with an auto insurance policy.

Auto insurance premiums are based on the driver's age, marital status (married or single), driving record (traffic tickets, accidents, etc.), and credit score (bills paid on time) as well as the type of car (sports cars are more expensive to insure), amount of coverage, and deductibles (amount you will pay to have repairs made). Auto insurance covers damage to your car (called collision), damage to someone else's car (called comprehensive), and personal liability (if someone sues you because the accident was your fault).

Auto insurance is provided by numerous companies and the insurance premiums for auto insurance vary greatly. Therefore, consider getting at least three auto insurance quotes. Make sure that all three quotes provide the same coverage.

Combining auto insurance, renter's or homeowner's insurance, and personal umbrella liability insurance with the same company may save money because the insurance company will generally give a discount for having all three policies with it. Therefore, compare the premiums for all three policies to determine which is the best buy. Exhibit 11B provides a sample insurance quote worksheet.

Renter's or Homeowner's Insurance. You will probably be renting (dorm or apartment) while you are a student and should consider purchasing renter's insurance, which would cover your possessions in the rented space against damage or theft and also provide liability insurance.

If you own a home, a homeowner's insurance policy would cover damage to your home (building) and possessions (furniture, clothing, electronic equipment, and jewelry). The insurance company will either repair the damage or replace the item if repair is not practical or if the property is stolen.

Homeowner's insurance also provides liability insurance to pay damages to people who might sue you as a result of visiting your home. For example, if a visitor slips on your steps and breaks a leg, the liability insurance would pay damages (up to the policy limits) to the person hurt, if it is determined that you are liable for the person's injuries.

A homeowner's policy is needed when you own a home (house, town home, or condo). The home mortgage company will require that you have adequate homeowner's insurance to either repair the property or to repay the loan if the property cannot be repaired.

A key point in purchasing renter's or homeowner's insurance is that the insurance coverage should replace any damaged or stolen property rather than just pay the depreciated value of the property. For example, a three-year old television which costs $300 is stolen. This three-year old television may only be worth $100 when stolen. However, a similar television would now cost $350. If you had replacement insurance, the insurance company would pay $350 to replace the television that was stolen. If the insurance coverage only pays the depreciated value of the television, then you would receive only $100.

A second point about property insurance is to not overinsure the property. Insurance premiums are based on the amount of insurance purchased, but the insurance company will only pay the actual amount of the loss.

For example, you buy a home for $125,000 with a land value of $25,000. Since land cannot be destroyed or stolen, there is no need to insure the land value of $25,000. The home should be insured for $100,000. If the home were insured for $150,000 and the home was destroyed, the insurance company would only pay $100,000, the value of the home. The insurance premium paid for the extra $50,000 of coverage is wasted and will provide no benefit if there is a loss; therefore, don't pay for something that isn't going to provide a benefit. Please note that property does increase in value and you may need to increase coverage to reflect the increase in value from year to year.

You don't want to be underinsured either, because the insurance company only pays up to the coverage amount selected. In the example above, if the home were insured for $75,000 and there was a complete loss, the insurance company would only pay $75,000 even though the cost to rebuild the home would be $100,000. Therefore, $25,000 would be lost because the home was underinsured. Property should be insured for its current value – no more and no less.

As mentioned earlier, you should purchase the renter's or homeowner's insurance, car insurance, and personal umbrella liability insurance from the same company to receive discounts on the insurance premiums. Exhibit 11B provides a sample insurance quote worksheet.

Personal Umbrella Liability Insurance. Consider purchasing a personal umbrella liability insurance policy, which is a liability policy used to pay someone who sues you for injury at your home or as a result of a car accident. Generally, a personal umbrella liability insurance policy increases the liability amount above the amounts in the auto and homeowner's insurance policies.

For example, if the auto insurance policy has a $300,000 liability limit and the homeowner's policy also has a $300,000 liability limit, then a personal umbrella liability insurance policy would provide insurance coverage above $300,000 by the amount selected – say $1,000,000. Therefore, the personal umbrella liability insurance policy would cover claims for damage between $300,000 and $1,300,000 or an additional $1,000,000. Although $1,300,000 is a lot of money, people have been sued and have had to pay large amounts for injuries. If you don't have this insurance, then any amounts above the $300,000 liability limit for the auto and homeowner's policy would come from your assets.

The insurance premium for this additional coverage is not very expensive and you should consider a personal umbrella liability insurance policy when you start to accumulate wealth. If sued for injuries on your property, you could end up having to sell all of your assets to pay the person for the injuries.

This insurance is also very helpful in that the insurance company will fight the claim for damages in court because they don't want to have to pay the $1,000,000 additional amount ($1,300,000 less the auto and homeowner's liability amount of $300,000).

As indicated earlier, you should purchase the personal umbrella liability insurance policy, the renter's or homeowner's insurance policy, and the car insurance policy from the same company to receive discounts on the insurance premiums. Exhibit 11B provides a sample insurance quote worksheet.

Insurance

Key Points

- Shop for the best insurance policy

    - Provides coverage required
    - Provides the lowest costs
    - Use employer-provided insurance when available

- Health insurance

    - A necessity
    - Insurance company discounts apply when you have to pay
    - Parents' health insurance may cover you while a full-time student

- Life insurance

    - Purchase whole life insurance when you are young
    - Purchase whole life insurance from a mutual insurance company, not a stock insurance company
    - Consider life insurance while you are a student

- Term life insurance provides temporary insurance

    - Less expensive than whole life insurance
    - No cash value
    - Provisions for shorter term needs

- Whole life insurance provides permanent insurance

    - More expensive than term life insurance
    - Builds cash value – net worth
    - Provisions for final medical and funeral expenses

- Disability insurance provides money when injured and unable to work

- Auto insurance

    - Premiums vary greatly
    - Compare at least three quotes
    - Parents' auto insurance policy may cover you while a full-time student

- Renter's or homeowner's insurance

    - Purchase renter's insurance while a student
    - Don't overinsure or underinsure your home

- Personal umbrella liability insurance protects your assets from liability lawsuits

- Combining auto, homeowner's (or renter's), and personal umbrella liability insurance polices with the same company may reduce your total premium

NOTES

Exhibit 11A – Comparison of Insurance Types

Page 1 of 2

Type of Insurance	Coverage
Health	Medical (doctors and hospitals) Medicines Dental
Life – Term	Death (pays cash at death)
Life – Whole	Death (pays cash at death)
Disability	Unable to work (pays cash)
Auto	Cars
Homeowner's	Home
Umbrella	Personal liability

Exhibit 11A - Comparison of Insurance Types

Page 2 of 2

Key Considerations

Co-payments – amount you pay for each visit
Deductibles – amount you pay
Increasing the deductible will lower the premiums
May be provided by employer

Less expensive than whole life
No cash surrender value
Cheaper the younger you are; premiums increase with age
May be provided by employer

More expensive than term life
Creates cash surrender value
Premium does not change

May be provided by employer

Must have for each car owned
Higher deductibles will reduce premiums
Combine with home insurance to reduce premiums

Higher deductibles will reduce premiums
Combine with auto insurance to reduce premiums

Combine with auto and home insurance to reduce premiums
Important to protect against lawsuits for damages

TOPAZ CONSULTING, LLC

Exhibit 11B - Insurance Quote Worksheet

Type of Coverage	Amount of Coverage	Annual Insurance Premiums		
		A	B	C
Auto Insurance (one car)				
Comprehensive - your car	Actual Value			
Collision - someone else's car	Actual Value			
Property Damage Liability	100,000			
Bodily Injury Liability				
Each Person	300,000			
Each Occurrence	300,000			
Medical Payments	1,000			
Uninsured Motorists - Bodily Injury				
Each Person	300,000			
Each Occurrence	300,000			
Annual Premium (6 month premium x 2)		610	785	650
Homeowner's Insurance				
Property Coverage				
Dwelling	250,000			
Other Structures	25,000			
Personal Property	175,000			
Loss of Use	250,000			
Liability Coverage				
Personal Liability	300,000			
Medical Payments	1,000			
Annual Premium (usually an annual premium)		450	475	395
Personal Umbrella Liability Insurance				
Excess Personal Liability	1,000,000			
Underlying Insurance Coverage				
Auto - Property Damage Liability	100,000			
Auto - Bodily Injury Liability	300,000			
Homeowner's - Personal Liability	300,000			
Annual Premium (usually an annual premium)		140	130	145
Total Annual Premium for all Policies		1,200	1,390	1,190

CHAPTER TWELVE
Car Purchase

For most people, selecting a car is similar to selecting a utility player on a sports team. A utility player and a car should be affordable, reliable, versatile, and easy to maintain.

There are many places to buy a car, even over the Internet. If you like to haggle, then buying a car should be fun because there are usually negotiations when buying a car – whether the car is new or used.

How Much Car Can You Afford? First, decide on how much you can afford to pay for a car. Generally, you will pay a down payment (from your savings) and will borrow the balance of the car purchase price and fees. Remember from Chapter Ten on debt management that the auto loan should not use the Rule of 78's to compute interest.

To determine how much you can afford to pay for a car, visit a bank or a credit union where the banker will review your financial situation and give advice about how much you can borrow and how much the monthly payments will be as well as any fees involved with an auto loan. Adding the down payment from savings to the amount that can be borrowed will equal the price that can be paid for the car.

Budget. Owning a car is expensive, but necessary for most people. Costs after the purchase include annual registration fees (state and perhaps local), personal property taxes, auto insurance premiums, repairs (hopefully a warranty will cover any major repair), maintenance (don't forget to change the oil), and, of course, fuel. Be sure that these items have been included in the budget so that you can pay bills on time and you can maintain a good credit rating. Exhibit 12A provides a sample annual car budget.

Type of Car and Options. After deciding how much you can pay, your search for the dream car can begin. Make a list of the features you desire – such as automatic transmission, air conditioning, and CD player. Then determine the make, model, year, color, and mileage of your dream car.

The Internet's used cars sites are a good place to start to see what is available for the price that you have decided to pay. The year the car was built and the number of miles on the car are major factors in determining the price of the car. Other sources to search for cars are local newspaper ads, local auto sale books, and new and used auto dealers.

Another consideration is whether to buy a new or used car. If you are considering purchasing a new car, investigate the purchase of a slightly used car which is still under the manufacturer's warranty. New cars depreciate (lose value) very quickly. Therefore, let someone else take the big depreciate hit and negotiate a good deal on a car that is about one year old with about 10,000 miles rather than a new car. You may be surprised by how much you can save and still enjoy the style of a newer car.

After you have selected the type of car, shop the various sources mentioned above to determine who has the best price on the car with the features wanted. Visit several car dealers to inspect the car and take a test drive to see how the car drives. You don't have to purchase a car just because you take a test drive.

Total Costs of the Car Purchase. In negotiating the purchase price, consider the appearance of the car (does it need a paint job?), the condition of the equipment (radio, air conditioning, etc.), the type of warranty (repairs that will be made to the car at no cost or at a small cost to you), and the dealer charges to sell the car – yes, there can be extra charges by the dealer in addition to the purchase price for the dealer to process the sale of the car.

Car value reference books (called "Blue Books") are available to assist you in determining the fair value of a car. Remember, you are looking for the best deal on the total cost to purchase the car, not just the purchase price for the car. Exhibit 12B provides a sample worksheet which outlines most of the cost of purchasing a car. Consider shopping at two or three car dealers to get the best overall deal.

When to Purchase a Car. During certain times of the year, car dealers have incentive programs to encourage customers to buy when cars are not selling at the rate they would like. A better price may be negotiated at the end of a month, when the dealer may be trying to meet a quota.

Also, when the model year is changing, usually in late summer, the car dealers try to sell all remaining new cars and used cars to make room for the new-year cars. When the new-year cars arrive, all existing cars become one year older and lower in price – remember the older a car is, the less valuable the car is.

Warranty. More than likely you will purchase the most expensive car that you can afford and thus cannot afford to pay for expensive car repairs. Therefore, it is important to understand the warranty on a used car. Unless the cost is outrageous, consider having at least a three year or 36,000 mile warranty, whichever occurs first, on a used car.

Sometimes this warranty can be negotiated as part of the purchase price. Other times, you must purchase this warranty, either from the dealer or from a car warranty company. Since a warranty can be an expensive item, shop for the best rate on the warranty.

Also consider the type of warranty. A bumper-to-bumper warranty covers everything and is the most expensive warranty to purchase. Other warranties may only cover the major components of the car (such as the engine and transmission) and will be less expensive.

Financing. Next, decide on financing the car purchase. You must determine the interest rate charged on the amount borrowed and any fees charged by the lender. Although most dealers provide "on premise financing," the dealer-provided loan may not be the best loan. Shop around (credit unions, banks, or maybe a home equity loan, if you own a home) to determine if there are better auto loans with lower interest rates and lower fees.

While having the dealer provide the car, the warranty, and the financing is very convenient, you may save money by buying the car from the dealer, buying the car warranty (if you have to pay for the warranty) from a warranty company, and borrowing the car loan amount from a credit union or bank.

Auto Insurance. You must purchase auto insurance before you drive the car from the car lot. If you have homeowner's or renter's insurance, contact the insurance company that is providing that insurance to get an auto insurance premium quote. Also, contact other auto insurance companies to get an insurance quote so that you can select the insurance company that provides the best price. (Chapter Eleven provides information regarding auto insurance.)

Registration and Property Taxes. After purchase, you must register the car with the locality and state where you live. Generally, the car dealer will take care of this for a fee. You may decide to register the car yourself to save the dealer's fee. But, you will still have to pay the local and state registration fees.

Also, you will probably have to pay personal property tax on the car. Annually, you may be required to file a personal property tax return. The local government determines the amount of tax, if any, that you must pay on the car. This tax is usually due either once or twice a year. Generally, the locality will send you a bill for the amount of personal property tax. You must purchase a state auto license annually. Some local governments also require that a decal be purchased annually for the car.

NOTES

Car Purchase
Key Points

- Decide how much you can afford to pay for a car

- Prepare a car budget

- Select the car that meets your needs and budget

- Investigate buying a slightly used car for the best car value

- Negotiate the best total price for the car

- Make sure that a used car has a good warranty

- Find the best financing possible

    - Lowest interest rate with the minimum up-front costs
    - Simple interest with no prepayment penalty

- Find the best deal on auto insurance

NOTES

Exhibit 12A - Annual Car Budget

Costs	Monthly Costs	Annual Costs
Car payment ($10,000 at 7% for 4 years)	239.46	2,873.52
Auto insurance premium		495.00
State license		45.00
County/City decal		20.00
Personal property taxes		200.00
Maintenance - oil changes, etc		100.00
Repairs		300.00
Gas	100.00	1,200.00
Total annual costs		5,233.52
Total monthly average costs		436.13

Note: Your costs will depend on your age, credit rating, driving record, where you live, the type of car, the condition of your car, and the miles you drive.

TOPAZ CONSULTING, LLC

Exhibit 12B - Costs of Purchasing a Car

Dealer costs

Price of car (negotiated)	10,000		
Processing fees	195		A
Other fees	-		
Total dealer costs		10,195	

Warranty - extended warranty if a used car   695   B
    Purchased from either the dealer
       or a warranty company

Local government costs

Sales tax (use 3% as an example)	300		
Title and registration fees	95		
Other fees	-		
Total local government fees		395	C

Total cost to purchase a car   11,285

A   Some dealers don't charge this fee. Therefore, a dealer that does not charge this fee may have a better overall deal.

B   Some dealers provide a limited warranty. This warranty is in addition to the dealer's warranty.

C   These costs are usually the same because they are based on where you live and not on where you purchased the car.

CHAPTER THIRTEEN
Taxes

There is an old saying that states, "The only sure things are death and taxes." Taxes are definitely here to stay. We have to pay for the services that our federal, state, and local governments provide, such as national defense, highways, public schools, police, fire, welfare payments to the needy, social security payments, and Medicare payments for health costs.

Examples of major taxes are income tax, social security tax, Medicare tax, sales tax, property tax, and excise tax. There are three major taxing authorities – federal, state, and local (cities and counties – called localities). You must pay your taxes or the government can sell your property in order to collect the taxes you owe. There are planning strategies – such as saving for retirement and buying a home – that will minimize your taxes.

Income Taxes. All three taxing authorities can require you to pay income tax. The federal income tax rates range from 0% to 35% for individuals. State income tax rates range from 0% to 11%, depending on your income. The local government may also have an income tax.

Generally, you must file a federal income tax return if your gross income is $8,450 or more. If federal income tax was withheld from your paycheck, you should file a federal income tax return to receive a refund, even if your gross income is less than $8,450. You will find the federal income tax rate schedules at Exhibit 13A. Additional information regarding federal income taxes can be found at the Internal Revenue Service (IRS) website (www.irs.gov).

Generally, income taxes are withheld from your paycheck based on your income and the allowances you claim. Federal Form W-4 must be filed with your employer to claim the federal allowances. Do not have too much income tax withheld because this results in an interest-free loan to the government. Your money should be earning interest in a savings or money market account (insured by the FDIC).

Most people have to file an income tax return once a year. On this return, report your income, claim any deductions you have (such as retirement contributions), claim either a standard deduction or itemized deductions (such as state and local income taxes, property taxes on your car and home, home mortgage interest, and charitable contributions), your exemptions, and any tax credits for which you qualify. If tax is due, you will have to send payment with the income tax return by the return due date. If you overpaid taxes, you will receive a tax refund.

To assist in the preparation of income tax returns, each employer will provide you with a Form W-2 which summarizes your earnings for the year and the taxes that have been withheld for the year. You may receive several Form 1099s, which report income from miscellaneous jobs (if you don't receive a Form W-2), interest, and dividends. For each home mortgage, you should receive a Form 1098, which reports the amount of interest paid for the year, as well as the amount of real estate taxes paid by the mortgage company for the year. The information provided on these forms must be included in the income tax return.

Most states do have income taxes. Some localities will also have an income tax. The states that do not have income taxes must have funds to operate; therefore, these states have either other taxes to raise revenue or higher tax rates on non-income items (such as higher sales and property tax rates than states that have income taxes).

Education Tax Credits. You may qualify for an education tax credit for qualified education expenses (tuition and certain related expenses). A tax credit reduces the amount of income tax that you must pay. If the education tax credit is more than the amount of tax owed for the year, the excess credit is not refunded. The tax credit can only reduce your income tax to zero. Further, the tax credit is claimed by the person who claims the student as a dependent. For example, if the parents claim the student as a dependent, then the parents would claim the tax credit on their income tax return.

There are two federal education tax credits, the Hope Credit and the Lifetime Learning Credit. For 2007, the maximum education tax credits were either $1,650 for the Hope Credit or $2,000 for the Lifetime Learning Credit.

The Hope Credit is equal to 100% of the first $1,100 of qualified education expenses, plus 50% of the next $1,100 of qualified education expenses (maximum Hope Credit is $1,650 for 2007). The credit is available for only the first two years of college. The student must be enrolled at least half time and be pursuing an undergraduate degree.

The Lifetime Learning Credit is equal to 20% of qualified education expenses up to $10,000 of qualified education expenses (maximum Lifetime Learning Credit is $10,000 x 20% = $2,000 for 2007). The credit is available anytime for college courses or courses to acquire or improve job skills. The student has only to be enrolled for one or more courses and does not need to be pursuing a degree.

The education tax credits begin to be reduced when the adjusted gross income is $47,000 or more ($94,000 or more if a joint return is filed). You may receive a higher tax benefit if you elect to deduct your qualified education expenses at higher income levels. IRS Publication 970, Tax Benefits for Education, provides more detail on education tax credits as well as information on other ways to reduce income taxes for education (www.irs.gov).

Social Security Tax. Only the federal government requires that you pay social security tax. Your employer is required to withhold social security tax from your paycheck in an amount equal to 6.2% of wages (up to a maximum of $97,500 in wages for 2007). This tax goes into a trust fund to provide retirement, survivors, and disability income for over 47 million people. There is no separate return due for social security tax.

After age sixty-two, you may be entitled to receive a retirement payment from Social Security. Nevertheless, these payments are not intended to pay the same amount that you were making before retirement; therefore, you will need a separate retirement plan to make up the shortfall in retirement income (see Chapter Six on savings).

There is concern that for younger workers, the Social Security system may not be able to pay all of its obligations. Consequently, Social Security payments may be reduced in the future which makes it even more important for you to save for retirement.

Medicare Tax. Like social security tax, only the federal government requires that you pay Medicare tax. Your employer is required to withhold Medicare tax from your paycheck in an amount equal to 1.45% of all of your wages (there is no maximum amount of wages for the Medicare tax). This tax goes into a trust fund to provide health care for retired and disabled people.

Like the social security tax, there is no separate return for Medicare tax. Again, there is concern that this trust fund will not meet its obligations in the future. Therefore, you also should consider establishing a savings program to provide for medical costs after retirement.

Sales Tax. There is no federal sales tax. State and local sales tax rates range from a combined state and local sales tax rate of 0% to 11%. Most people are familiar with sales tax. Sales tax is the tax you pay when you purchase items such as groceries (unless groceries are exempt - not taxed), clothes, appliances, and cars.

You do not have to file sales tax returns (unless an item – such as furniture – is purchased out of state and brought into your home state). The store where an item is purchased collects the sales tax and sends the sales tax to the government.

Property Tax. Property is generally left to the local governments (cities and counties) to tax. This tax is based on the property a person owns – such as cars, homes, and furniture. Generally, a property tax return is filed with the locality each year. The locality will then determine how much property tax is due for the year. Depending on the locality, this tax may be paid in one payment (say in December of each year) or in two payments (say in June and December of each year).

Generally, the largest property tax is the tax paid on a home (called real estate taxes). Renters effectively pay real estate taxes because the rent payment includes the real estate taxes paid by the owner of the rental unit.

Excise Tax. Excise tax can be collected by the federal, state, and local governments and range greatly in amount based on the type of item purchased. It is similar to sales tax in that it is charged on items purchased. The difference between the two taxes is that you do not see the amount of the excise tax because it is included in the price of the item.

For example, the price you pay for gasoline will include a federal excise tax of $0.184 per gallon and a state excise tax from about $0.075 to about $0.31 per gallon. Generally, you pay only excise tax on gasoline (you do not pay sales tax on gasoline purchases). But, some states do charge both a sales and excise tax on gasoline. Other items that include an excise tax in the price you pay are cigarettes, liquor, wine, and beer.

Other Taxes. There are probably other taxes in the area where you live. Determine the tax rules with the state and local governments where you live in order to make sure that you pay the proper tax when it is due. Otherwise, you would be subject to interest and late payment penalties, in addition to the tax.

Final Comments. You must pay taxes and they take a significant amount of your income. Be aware that you need to estimate the amount of income after taxes (income, social security, and Medicare tax) when planning your budgets.

For example, in 2006 if you were single and you earned $30,000, your net after-tax pay would be about $23,350 if you lived in a state with a state income tax rate of 5% (federal income tax = $2,855; social security tax = $1,860; Medicare tax = $435; and state income tax = $1,500).

Remember to budget for other tax payments such as property tax (car and real estate). These taxes can be significant, and you want to be sure to plan to make these tax payments on time. If you have a home mortgage, the monthly mortgage payment will probably include a payment for the real estate taxes. If it does, then the lender will be responsible for paying the real estate taxes on the home when the taxes are due.

Sales tax is included in the total costs of an item. A $500 purchase may actually cost $550 (including a 10% sales tax). This is especially true for major purchases (such as a car) where the tax is computed on the entire purchase price. For example, a car that cost $20,000 would actually cost $21,200 with a 6% sales tax.

Managing taxes is just like managing any other cost of living. You should determine the amount of taxes and the due date for taxes to avoid any unpleasant surprises by having to pay taxes you were not expecting.

This guide is not intended to give tax advice and should only be used as a reminder to consider taxes in your financial planning. The above examples illustrate how a tax might work and is not intended to be a computation of the exact amount of tax that you might pay. Tax rates and items that are taxed are subject to change (and they usually do change) by the federal, state, and local governments at any time.

NOTES

Taxes
Key Points

- You must pay taxes or the government can sell your property

- Do not have too much income taxes withheld; put the additional take home pay in a savings account

- Social Security will not provide all of the income needed for retirement; establish a separate retirement plan

- Include all taxes in budgets so that you avoid tax payment surprises

NOTES

Exhibit 13A - Federal Income Tax Rate Schedules

2006 Federal Income Tax Rate Schedules

Schedule X - Single

If taxable income is over ---	But not over ---	The tax is:
0	7,550	10% of the amount over 0
7,550	30,650	755 plus 15% of the amount over 7,550
30,650	74,200	4,220 plus 25% of the amount over 30,650
74,200	154,800	15,108 plus 28% of the amount over 74,200
154,800	336,550	37,676 plus 33% of the amount over 154,800
336,550	no limit	97,653 plus 35% of the amount over 336,550

Schedule Y-1 - Married Filing Jointly

If taxable income is over ---	But not over ---	The tax is:
0	15,100	10% of the amount over 0
15,100	61,300	1,510 plus 15% of the amount over 15,100
61,300	123,700	8,440 plus 25% of the amount over 61,300
123,700	188,450	24,040 plus 28% of the amount over 123,700
188,450	336,550	42,170 plus 33% of the amount over 188,450
336,550	no limit	91,043 plus 35% of the amount over 336,550

Schedule Y-2 - Married Filing Separately

If taxable income is over ---	But not over ---	The tax is:
0	7,550	10% of the amount over 0
7,550	30,650	755 plus 15% of the amount over 7,550
30,650	61,850	4,220 plus 25% of the amount over 30,650
61,850	94,225	12,020 plus 28% of the amount over 61,850
94,225	168,275	21,085 plus 33% of the amount over 94,225
168,275	no limit	45,522 plus 35% of the amount over 168,275

NOTES

CHAPTER FOURTEEN
Credit Management

One of the best ways to improve your financial well being is to manage your credit rating. When borrowing to purchase items, your credit rating will determine how much you can borrow and how much the loan will cost. Your credit rating also comes into play when you apply for a credit card, buy insurance, or apply for certain jobs. This chapter explains how your credit rating works and highlights some of the steps you should take to enhance your credit rating.

Importance of Credit Rating. Everyone needs to borrow money on occasions to pay for major purchases, such as a car or home, or to pay for an emergency. Today, credit cards are a convenient way to purchase everyday items for most people. The better your credit rating, the less you pay to borrow money.

For example, the interest rate for an auto loan may be at 6% interest if a person has a good credit rating rather than at 9% interest if the person has a bad credit rating. The reason for the lower interest rate is because the lender believes that a person with a good credit rating will be more likely to make the auto loan payments on time each month. In other words, the person is a good credit risk, and the lender is willing to charge a lower interest rate.

Some insurance companies also use credit ratings to determine the insurance premiums they charge for auto insurance. The higher the credit rating, the more likely a person is to pay the insurance premiums on time. A higher credit rating may indicate that the person is more responsible and would be a better driver, which presents less of a risk to the insurance company. Therefore, the insurance company will charge a lower insurance premium for someone with a higher credit rating.

Employers may also use credit ratings to determine if an employee pays financial obligations in a timely manner, which means that he or she is reliable and can be trusted with company responsibilities. This trust is especially important when the employee moves up in a company.

Consequently, a bad credit rating will result in more expensive loans (higher fees and interest rates) and may even result in not being able to borrow for the items needed. Further, auto insurance may be more expensive and a person may be denied a job because of a bad credit rating.

Credit Rating. In the past, determining your own credit rating was almost impossible. But today, we have access to information that helps manage our credit rating. Free credit reports are available from the three major credit bureaus. These credit reports are used to determine a person's credit rating, which is commonly known today as a credit score.

Credit Reports. You can obtain a credit report from each of the three major credit bureaus once a year for no charge. In order to monitor credit all year, you may wish to stagger the request for the free credit reports so that you receive a credit report from one of the credit bureaus after each four month period (perhaps one in February, one in June and one in October).

Request your free credit report from any of the three major credit bureaus by going to www.annualcreditreport.com or by contacting each credit bureau as indicated in Exhibit 14A.

The credit report generally provides four types of information – (i) identifying (name, social security number, driver's license number, addresses, date of birth, employer, and spouse's name); (ii) credit history (all credit accounts, dated opened, credit limit, outstanding balance, late or missed payments, if someone else is on the account, etc.); (iii) inquiries (list of all of inquiries for your credit history, including inquiries from credit card companies, lenders, service providers, landlords, and insurance companies); and (iv) public records (the information that is available to the public, such as bankruptcy, tax liens, foreclosures, and court judgments).

Review the credit report carefully to be sure that it is accurate. If you find errors, notify the credit bureau immediately and also notify the company that may have reported the incorrect information to the credit bureau. If you suspect identity theft, follow the steps outlined in Chapter Fifteen on identity theft.

Some of the items that credit reports do not include are income, medical history, level of education, gender, religion, national origin, investment accounts, savings accounts, and information on purchases made with cash or a check.

Access to a credit report is limited to people and companies that have a legitimate purpose. For example, potential lenders (home mortgage and auto loans), credit card companies, insurance companies, employers, and landlords can have access to your credit report. Of course, you can authorize anyone to have access to your credit report by giving them written permission.

Please note that a free credit report does not provide your credit score. You will need to pay a fee to get the credit score as explained next.

Credit Score. Since most credit reports are several pages long, the lending industry prefers to use the credit score, which is a three-digit number summary of the credit report. Credit scores range from 300 to 850, depending on which credit bureau is calculating the score. The higher the credit score, the better the credit. Using this three digit number, a person's credit will be classified as poor, fair, good, or excellent.

Credit scores are computed by giving a weight to each aspect of the credit report. For example, paying bills on time may have a weight of 35% of the total score, the ratio of debt to credit limit may account for 30% of the credit score, the length of time of a credit history may be 15%, the number of recently opened accounts may be 10%, and the type of loans may make up the remaining 10% of the credit score. Some models for computing credit scores may use other factors such as employment stability, debt-to-income ratios, and loan-to-value ratios.

You really do control your credit score by the actions you take to manage credit (unless your identity is stolen as explained in Chapter Fifteen on identity theft).

Pay Bills on Time. The most important thing to do to improve and/or maintain a credit score is to pay bills on time. Not only will you avoid late payment charges, you will avoid having a late payment reported to the credit bureaus, which will lower your credit score.

Paying bills on time means that you pay the amount currently due by the due date. For example, you use a credit card to pay for a major auto repair. When the credit card bill arrives, you don't have enough cash to pay the credit card in full. However, you do have enough cash to pay the minimum payment required. If you pay the minimum amount before the due date, the payment is not considered late. Of course, you will pay the credit card interest rate until you pay the credit card balance in full, but your credit score has been preserved for this aspect of the score.

Stay Well within Credit Limits. The second most important aspect in determining a credit score is the percent of the credit limit that has been used. This is called a utilization ratio. For example, if a credit card has a credit limit of $5,000 and a current balance of $2,000, the utilization ratio would be 40% ($2,000/$5,000).

Typically, the utilization ratio should be below 30% to 50%, depending on which company uses the credit score. Generally, having a credit balance of more than 70% of the credit limit is very harmful to a credit score. Therefore, "maxing" out credit cards (the outstanding balance is equal to the credit limit) is very bad for a credit score.

To reduce the utilization ratio, either pay down some of your credit balance or increase your credit limit. In the above example, if you paid $500 on the credit card, the outstanding balance would be $1,500 and the utilization ratio would now be 30% rather than 40%. Likewise, if you increase the credit limit to $7,000 and the outstanding balance remains at $2,000, the utilization ratio will drop to about 29%.

Another way to increase the utilization ratio is to apply for another credit card. The credit limit on the new card would increase the total credit limit because the computation is based on all of the credit cards and not on a card-by-card basis. However, try to keep the number of credit cards to no more than two or three. Also, you must make the minimum payment each month on each credit card or you will do more damage to your credit score by having late payments than by having a higher utilization ratio.

The basis of the utilization ratio is the outstanding balance at the time the lender requests the credit score. A high outstanding balance at the time of the credit score request will negatively affect the utilization ratio. Therefore, if you are planning to borrow for a home or an auto, you should delay major purchases on the credit cards, even if you plan to pay the credit card balance in full before the due date.

Length of Credit History. In computing your credit score, the length of time you have had credit is important. For example, the longer you have a credit card (and made your payments on time), the higher your credit score. Therefore, you may wish to keep older credit cards rather than applying for new ones every couple of years and canceling the older cards.

Of course, if the newer cards have better terms, then you may wish to go with the new card and perhaps keep the older card with minimal use. Remember, there should not be a fee to use a credit card (see Chapter Ten on debt management for more information about credit card features).

Credit Applications. The number of credit applications affects the credit score. Since more applications negatively affect the credit score, don't apply for excessive credit cards, including store credit cards. Again, you should only have the credit accounts that you need to accomplish your goals.

A big marketing tool today is to provide free interest on major purchases for a period of time. In order to qualify for the free interest, you usually have to complete a credit application. This application will most likely increase your number of credit applications and have a negative effect on your credit score.

Likewise, newer credit accounts lower the average age of the accounts. Remember, the longer the credit history, the better the credit score.

Types of Loans. The final factor in determining the credit score is the type of outstanding loans. Certain types of lenders are considered lenders of last resort and could hurt your credit score. The key is to know the company you are dealing with and to be sure that you can make payments on time.

Improving Your Credit Score. The best ways to improve your credit score are (i) pay bills on time, (ii) pay down credit card balances (also removes high interest debt), and (iii) maintain a good utilization ratio (the amount borrowed compared to the credit limit).

Denied Credit. If you are denied credit, you have a right to know the name and address of the credit bureau that supplied the credit report the lender used in denying credit. You also have the right to a free copy of the credit report that was used to deny credit. Review this credit report for errors and have all errors corrected by working with the credit bureau that issued the credit report.

Identity Theft. A very important part of managing credit is avoiding identity theft. If you become the victim of identity theft, you must take quick action to minimize the damage and to have credit records corrected. Chapter Fifteen on identity theft provides more details on steps to protect yourself and to manage the process of having credit records corrected.

Keeping Good Credit. As you can see from the above discussion, it is important to maintain good credit in order to minimize the costs of borrowing money. Maintaining a monthly budget (as explained in Chapter Sixteen) is the best way to stay on top of payments so that you make payments on time, as well as to signal if your spending is getting out of control.

NOTES

Credit Management

Key Points

- Credit rating can determine

  - Cost of borrowing money
  - Insurance premiums
  - Employment

- Credit reports

  - Request free report annually from three major credit bureaus
  - Review for accuracy and potential identity theft
  - Access to report limited to legitimate purposes
  - Does not include credit score

- Credit score

  - Fee required to receive credit score
  - Three digit number used by lenders to indicate your score

- Credit score components

  - Paying bills on time
  - Utilization ratio (amount borrowed / credit limit)
  - Length of credit history
  - Number of credit applications (fewer is better)
  - Types of loans

- Improving your credit score

  - Pay bills on time
  - Pay down credit card debt
  - Maintain good utilization ratio (30% to 50%)

    - Pay down debt
    - Increase credit limits

- Denial of your credit application

  - Entitled to free credit report used to deny credit
  - Check report for errors and have errors corrected

- Monthly budget helps to keep good credit rating

  - Helps pay bills on time
  - Signals if spending is getting out of control

Exhibit 14A – Credit Bureaus

EQUIFAX

    Order Credit Report: 1-800-685-1111
    Report Fraud: 1-800-525-6285
    www.equifax.com

EXPERIAN

    Order Credit Report: 1-888-397-3742
    Report Fraud: 1-888-397-3742
    www.experian.com

TRANSUNION

    Order Credit Report: 1-800-916-8800
    Report Fraud: 1-800-680-7289
    www.transunion.com

To request free credit report from all three credit bureaus go to:

    www.annualcreditreport.com

NOTES

CHAPTER FIFTEEN
Identity Theft

You need to pitch a shut out against identity thieves. By concentrating on every pitch (every financial transaction), you should be able to keep identity thieves from scoring. They may get on base (get your phone number or email address), but don't let them have your financial information so that they can score at your expense.

No matter how well you are pitching, sometimes you will tire on the mound (be scammed by a con artist) or someone on your team will make an error (unintentionally gives out your financial information). The identity thieves start a rally, but you need to stop the rally immediately by bringing in your closer to shut them down by notifying the credit bureaus, the companies affected, and the local police of the identity theft, and by closing accounts accessed by the thieves.

Identity theft is a growing concern and can harm your financial health. A thief can either take over an existing account or use your social security number to obtain new accounts in your name. If your identity is stolen, you may spend months, if not years, trying to undo the damage caused by the identity theft. Therefore, do all you can to prevent your identity from being stolen and used to make purchases in your name.

Effect of Identity Theft. Assume someone uses your name, social security number, and address to get credit cards. Then, he/she uses these credit cards to make purchases. Since the credit cards are in your name, the credit card company expects you to pay for these purchases.

When you don't make payments as required, probably because you are unaware of the credit card, the credit card companies notify the credit bureaus that payments are delinquent. When you apply for credit, the credit bureaus report that you have a low credit score because you have not made required payments. As a result of this low credit score, you will be either denied credit or charged a much higher interest rate.

Personal Information. Consider keeping your personal financial information such as your social security card, bank statements, credit card statements, and other documents in a place that is only accessible by you. Maintain in a secure place a list of account numbers and phone numbers (credit card companies, banks, credit bureaus, etc.) so that you can immediately contact companies if you become a victim of identity theft.

Mail. Collect mail as soon as possible from the mailbox. If you are going to be out of town for a few days, have the post office hold your mail until you return. Identity thieves can obtain personal information from the mail you receive (credit card statements and bank statements) and you don't want them to have a lot of time to take your mail.

Shred Documents. Consider shredding documents that contain personal information before throwing them in the trash. Someone could easily go through the trash looking for personal information such as credit card statements, bills, and bank statements.

Social Security Card. Your social security card should not be carried in your wallet or purse and you should never disclose your social security number to anyone, unless required by law. Your social security number is one of the key items a thief uses to steal your identity.

Checks. Never print your social security number on checks. Consider having only your initials printed on the checks. If someone should steal the checks, they would not know how you sign the checks (with initials, first name, or middle name). Also, do not put your home phone number (perhaps use your work phone number) on checks. If you have a post office box, consider using the post office box address rather than your home address on the checks.

Writing Checks. Include only the minimum amount of information on a check. For example, when paying a credit card, include the last four digits of the credit card number. Never write your social security number on a check. Use some other form of identification, if the person accepting your check requires identification.

Credit Cards. You should sign a new or replacement credit card on the back immediately upon receipt. Credit cards should be kept in a secure place where you would know if they were missing. Credit cards should not be used as identification and never leave a credit card with someone as a security deposit. Your credit card number should be given over the telephone only when you initiate the call and you are sure that you are dealing with a valid business.

Telephone. Do not give out personal information to anyone who calls on the phone. The person may be an identity thief posing as a person from a legitimate business with which you deal.

Internet. Do not give out personal information in response to an email. Identity thieves use the Internet to deceive people (called phishing) into disclosing their social security number, credit card numbers, bank account information, passwords, and other personal information about financial affairs.

Phishers will send an email or pop-up message that claims to be from your bank, online payment service, government agency, or other business with which you deal. The message will request that you update or validate your account information and may actually threaten some action against you if you don't respond.

The Federal Trade Commission (FTC) suggests that you not reply or click on the link in any message that requests personal or financial information. Legitimate companies do not ask for this information by email. Further, do not email personal or financial information because email is not a secure method of sending information.

Monitor Accounts. In order to catch identity theft quickly, monitor all of your accounts at least monthly. When your bank statement arrives, reconcile the account immediately to determine if there have been any unauthorized charges such as checks you didn't write, ATM withdrawals that you didn't make, debit charges for purchases you didn't make, debit charges to pay bills that are not your bills, or any other charge that you did not authorize.

When a credit card statement arrives, review the statement immediately for any charges that you did not authorize. Likewise, review any other financial statements that you receive to ensure that only activity that you authorized is on the statements. If you have Internet access to accounts, check accounts routinely to determine if there have been any unauthorized charges to the accounts. If you find an item on a statement that you did not authorize, you should immediately notify the company that has the account.

Pay attention to billing cycles. If a bill does not arrive at the usual time, follow up with the creditor to be sure that a thief has not stolen your identity and changed your address so that you will not receive the bill with the unauthorized charges.

Credit Reports. You can obtain your credit reports from each of the three major credit bureaus once a year for no charge. Exhibit 14A lists the three major credit bureaus. In order to monitor your credit all year, stagger your request for the free credit reports from the three credit bureaus. For example, order the credit report from TransUnion in February, Equifax in June, and Experian in October.

After you receive a credit report, be sure to completely review the report for any unusual or unauthorized accounts and balances. If you discover any incorrect or unauthorized information, contact the credit bureaus immediately to correct the information. You should also contact the company that supplied the incorrect or unauthorized information to the credit bureaus to correct the information.

If Your Identity is Stolen. You should notify the three credit bureaus immediately to place a fraud alert on your name and social security number (this service is free) if your identity is stolen. Exhibit 14A provides information on the three credit bureaus.

File a report with the local police where the identity theft occurred. Keep a copy of the report because you may need the report to make claims to creditors.

Review all accounts and report any unauthorized charges on your accounts to the company that has the account (credit card companies, banks, etc.). Close any account that has unauthorized use and open a new account.

Finally, file a complaint with the Federal Trade Commission (FTC) toll-free at 1-877-IDTHEFT (1-877-438-4338). The FTC web site (www.ftc.gov) provides more information on identity theft and provides sample forms to assist you in recovering from identity theft.

NOTES

Identity Theft

Key Points

- Protect your social security number

- Collect mail as soon as possible

- Shred financial documents before discarding

- Print minimum amount of information on checks

- Do not give out personal or financial information to persons who contact you by phone or Internet

- Monitor accounts at least monthly

- Request free credit reports once a year

- If your identity is stolen

  - Close accounts affected and open new accounts
  - Notify credit bureaus
  - File a report with the local police
  - Notify companies that have the accounts of the unauthorized transactions
  - File a complaint with the Federal Trade Commission

NOTES

CHAPTER SIXTEEN
Budgets

Budgets are financial road maps to help you manage your finances. If you compare actual numbers with the budget numbers, you will be able to identify quickly if you are meeting financial goals or if you are getting into financial trouble by over-spending. If you have never prepared a budget, now is a great time to start.

Key Elements. The key elements to a budget are income, taxes, savings, expenses, and net balance (either positive or negative). The budget should cover a calendar year because some items may only occur once or twice a year – such as college tuition and property taxes.

Condensed Budgets. Exhibit 16A provides a sample of a condensed annual budget and Exhibit 16B provides a sample of a condensed monthly budget. These condensed budgets show the cash received (after all deductions) and the cash payments without identifying all of the income and expense items. The condensed budget is used to track, on a monthly basis, your cash flow (the cash received minus the cash spent) and not your total income.

The monthly budget format is a good tool to use to be sure that you make payments on time because it lists each company you have to pay. It also provides a way to compare the budget with actual income and expenses, which will highlight any differences.

Detailed Budgets. Exhibit 16C provides a sample of a detailed annual budget and Exhibit 16D provides a sample of a detailed monthly budget. These detailed budgets show all income and expenses on a gross basis (before any deductions) and are used to track all income and expenses. These budgets show the type of income and expense, but not necessarily the name of the company.

For example, the condensed budget would only show net take-home pay (actual cash you received); the detailed budget would show total salary, the taxes withheld from your paycheck, and other deductions from your paycheck (such as savings that were direct deposited to a savings plan).

Likewise, the condensed budget would show credit card payments rather than separating the credit card payments into different expense items such as groceries, travel, and entertainment.

Of course, these are just examples and you can decide how much detail to include in your budget. What is important is that you have a budget which helps you compare your budget to actual spending.

Income. No one seems to have enough income, especially college students. Nevertheless, we all must live within our means, which is defined as how much income we have. Income for budget purposes includes salary, bonuses, gifts, interest on savings and money market accounts, income from extra jobs, and any other income (scholarships and grants) that comes your way.

Since most students must borrow for college expenses, include your student loans as income for this budget since a significant part of your expenses may be paid with loans. Generally, student loans are not repaid until after graduation. Therefore, you do not need to budget a student loan payment while attending college.

Only budget the income that you are fairly certain to receive in order to avoid a shortfall. For example, you probably should not budget $50 an hour for your summer job. If you do have a shortfall in income, then you will need a student loan to assist with your college expenses. The budget will assist you in determining how much of a student loan is needed.

Taxes. Only budget for taxes that reduce your wages (income tax, social security tax, and Medicare tax) and that require a separate payment (property taxes). You should include other taxes, such as sales tax and excise tax, in the cost of the items purchased.

Savings. Be sure to budget for savings when you are working. Have money deposited directly into a savings plan by your employer (see Chapter Six on savings).

Expenses. Your college website will give you an estimate of the various costs to attend the college and is a great place to start to pull together your budget information for expenses. You will need to add your personal expenses to determine the total amount of money will need to attend college.

As a college student, you will have an option to live on campus and pay the college for room and board or to live off campus and incur the costs associated with apartment living, such as rent, utilities, and groceries. The budget exhibits assume that you live on campus, but also list the types of expenses you might incur if you live off campus.

Generally, not controlling spending is what causes people to get into financial trouble. Understanding and controlling spending are the main reasons for budgeting. Income, taxes, and savings can be estimated fairly accurately. However, spending can be drastically different from the budget amount. Also, by preparing a budget for an entire year, you can determine which month (or months) may have an increase in spending and can save enough in the other normal spending months to cover these more expensive months.

At the beginning of each semester, your monthly spending will be increased to cover the payments for tuition, room and board, books, and school supplies. To manage these twice-a-year payments, you must save during the period of time you are working. Plan to fund these expenses through savings, scholarships, grants, gifts from parents, and student loans.

Don't forget those once-a-year major payments such as property taxes and insurance payments. Perhaps some of these once-a-year payments can be converted to monthly payments to help manage these expenses.

Most car insurance companies permit car insurance premiums to be paid monthly rather than having to save to pay an annual premium all at one time. Please note that there is usually a fee to make monthly instead of annual payments.

As with all things in life, the easier you make something to do, the more likely you will follow through. Develop a budget that you understand and can maintain so that you can plan your financial affairs to avoid any unpleasant surprises. The key is to compare actual spending to the budget amount on a monthly basis so that you can change your spending, if necessary, before spending gets out of control.

Reminder. As discussed in Chapter Five on paying bills, many of the recurring payments (those that are due on the same day of each month and have the same amount due each month) may be paid automatically from your checking account. Car loan payments and insurance payments are ideal for automatic payment.

Please be sure to put automatic payments in your check register on the date paid so that you do not inadvertently overdraw the checking account. You must have cash in the checking account to pay the automatic payments as scheduled.

NOTES

Budgets

Key Points

- Key budget elements are income, taxes, savings, and expenses

- Prepare annual and monthly budgets

- Compare actual income and expenses with the budget amount each month

- Include student loans as part of your income

- Budget for taxes withheld from your wages and property taxes

- Budget highlights when major payments are due such as college tuition

- Convert annual payments to monthly payments (i.e., car insurance premiums)

- Save during the year for major one-time annual expenses

TOPAZ CONSULTING, LLC

Exhibit 16A - Condensed Annual Budget
Income and Expense Listed
by Net Amounts Received and by Company Paid

Page 1 of 2

	JAN	FEB	MAR	APR	MAY
Net cash from paycheck	-	-	-	-	-
Interest income (savings)	-	-	-	-	-
Scholarships and grants	1,500	-	-	-	-
Gift from parents	2,000	-	500	300	300
Student Loans	4,500	-	-	-	-
Total income received	8,000	-	500	300	300
Property taxes	-	-	-	-	-
Total taxes paid	-	-	-	-	-
Savings	-	-	-	-	-
Total savings	-	-	-	-	-
* College payment	7,250	-	-	-	-
* Apartment rent	-	-	-	-	-
* Electricity	-	-	-	-	-
* Gas - home	-	-	-	-	-
* Water & sewer	-	-	-	-	-
* Refuse pick up	-	-	-	-	-
* Telephone - home	-	-	-	-	-
* Internet	-	-	-	-	-
* Cable	-	-	-	-	-
Health insurance	48	48	48	48	48
Telephone - cell	53	53	53	53	53
Auto loan payment	-	-	-	-	-
Auto insurance	40	40	40	40	40
Life insurance	185	-	-	-	-
Cash	30	35	40	50	35
Credit card	80	125	270	110	75
Other					
Total other expenses	436	301	451	301	251
Net cash balance (cash shortfall)	314	(301)	49	(1)	49

* If student lives off campus, then substitute these items for the room and board costs paid to the college.

Exhibit 16A - Condensed Annual Budget
Income and Expense Listed
by Net Amounts Received and by Company Paid

Page 2 of 2

JUN	JUL	AUG	SEP	OCT	NOV	DEC	Total
1,478	1,478	1,478	-	-	-	-	4,434
-	5	5	7	5	3	3	28
-	2,000	-	-	-	-	-	3,500
-	-	-	-	-	100	100	3,300
-	3,500	-	-	-	-	-	8,000
1,478	6,983	1,483	7	5	103	103	19,262
-	-	-	-	-	-	100	100
-	-	-	-	-	-	100	100
1,100	(100)	300	(400)	(200)	(300)	(400)	-
1,100	(100)	300	(400)	(200)	(300)	(400)	-
-	6,700	550	-	-	-	-	14,500
-	-	-	-	-	-	-	-
-	-	-	-	-	-	-	-
-	-	-	-	-	-	-	-
-	-	-	-	-	-	-	-
-	-	-	-	-	-	-	-
-	-	-	-	-	-	-	-
-	-	-	-	-	-	-	-
48	48	48	48	48	48	48	576
53	53	53	53	53	53	53	636
-	-	-	-	-	-	-	-
40	40	40	40	40	40	40	480
-	-	-	-	-	-	-	185
60	65	70	45	35	25	75	565
185	155	450	255	75	185	185	2,150
-	-	-	-	-	-	-	-
386	361	661	441	251	351	401	4,592
(8)	22	(28)	(34)	(46)	52	2	70

TOPAZ CONSULTING, LLC

Exhibit 16B - Condensed Monthly Budget
Income & Expense Listed
by Net Amounts Received and by Company Paid

	January		
	Budget	Actual	Over (Under) Budget
Net cash from paycheck	-	-	-
Interest income (savings)	-	-	-
Scholarships and grants	1,500	1,500	-
Gift from parents	2,000	2,000	-
Student loans	4,500	4,500	-
Total income received	8,000	8,000	-
Property taxes			-
Total taxes paid	-	-	-
Savings	-	-	-
Total savings	-	-	-
* College payment	7,250	7,147	(103)
* Apartment rent	-	-	-
* Electricity	-	-	-
* Gas - home	-	-	-
* Water & sewer	-	-	-
* Refuse pick up	-	-	-
* Telephone - home	-	-	-
* Internet	-	-	-
* Cable	-	-	-
Health insurance	48	48	-
Telephone - cell	53	57	4
Auto loan payment	-	-	-
Auto insurance	40	40	-
Life insurance	185	185	-
Cash	30	45	15
Credit card	80	128	48
Other	-	-	-
Total other expenses	436	503	67
Net cash balance (cash shortfall)	314	350	36

   *   If student lives off campus, then substitute these items for the room and board costs paid to the college.

NOTES

TOPAZ CONSULTING, LLC

Exhibit 16C - Detailed Annual Budget
Income and Expense Listed by Type of Income and Expense

Page 1 of 2

	JAN	FEB	MAR	APR	MAY
Salary	-	-	-	-	-
Interest income (savings)	-	-	-	-	-
Scholarships and grants	1,500	-	-	-	-
Gift from parents	2,000	-	500	300	300
Student loans	4,500	-	-	-	-
Total income received	8,000	-	500	300	300
Taxes withheld on paycheck	-	-	-	-	-
Property taxes	-	-	-	-	-
Total taxes paid	-	-	-	-	-
Savings	-	-	-	-	-
Total savings	-	-	-	-	-
College Expenses					
Tuition	3,500	-	-	-	-
* Room and Board	3,200	-	-	-	-
Computer	-	-	-	-	-
Books	400	-	-	-	-
Supplies	150	-	-	-	-
Total college expenses	7,250	-	-	-	-
* Apartment rent	-	-	-	-	-
* Electricity	-	-	-	-	-
* Gas - home	-	-	-	-	-
* Water & sewer	-	-	-	-	-
* Refuse pick up	-	-	-	-	-
* Telephone - home	-	-	-	-	-
* Internet	-	-	-	-	-
* Cable	-	-	-	-	-
* Groceries	-	-	-	-	-
Health insurance	48	48	48	48	48
Telephone - cell	53	53	53	53	53
Auto loan payment	-	-	-	-	-
Auto insurance	40	40	40	40	40
Auto - gasoline	60	60	60	60	60
Auto maintenance	-	50	-	-	-
Life insurance	185	-	-	-	-
Clothes	-	-	200	-	-
Recreation (meals out, etc.)	50	50	50	100	50
Christmas gifts	-	-	-	-	-
Other	-	-	-	-	-
Total other expenses	436	301	451	301	251
Net cash balance (cash shortfall)	314	(301)	49	(1)	49

* If student lives off campus, then substitute these items for the room and board costs paid to the college.

160

Exhibit 16C - Detailed Annual Budget
Income and Expense Listed by Type of Income and Expense

Page 2 of 2

JUN	JUL	AUG	SEP	OCT	NOV	DEC	Total
1,600	1,600	1,600	-	-	-	-	4,800
-	5	5	7	5	3	3	28
-	2,000	-	-	-	-	-	3,500
-	-	-	-	-	100	100	3,300
-	3,500	-	-	-	-	-	8,000
1,600	7,105	1,605	7	5	103	103	19,628
122	122	122	-	-	-	-	366
-	-	-	-	-	-	100	100
122	122	122	-	-	-	100	466
1,100	(100)	300	(400)	(200)	(300)	(400)	-
1,100	(100)	300	(400)	(200)	(300)	(400)	-
-	3,500	-	-	-	-	-	7,000
-	3,200	-	-	-	-	-	6,400
-	-	-	-	-	-	-	-
-	-	400	-	-	-	-	800
-	-	150	-	-	-	-	300
-	6,700	550	-	-	-	-	14,500
-	-	-	-	-	-	-	-
-	-	-	-	-	-	-	-
-	-	-	-	-	-	-	-
-	-	-	-	-	-	-	-
-	-	-	-	-	-	-	-
-	-	-	-	-	-	-	-
48	48	48	48	48	48	48	576
53	53	53	53	53	53	53	636
-	-	-	-	-	-	-	-
40	40	40	40	40	40	40	480
120	120	120	60	60	60	60	900
25	-	-	190	-	-	-	265
-	-	-	-	-	-	-	185
-	-	300	-	-	-	-	500
100	100	100	50	50	50	100	850
-	-	-	-	-	100	100	200
-	-	-	-	-	-	-	-
386	361	661	441	251	351	401	4,592
(8)	22	(28)	(34)	(46)	52	2	70

TOPAZ CONSULTING, LLC

Exhibit 16D - Detailed Monthly Budget
Income and Expense Listed by Type of Income and Expense

	January		
	Budget	Actual	Over (Under) Budget
Salary	-	-	-
Interest income (savings)	-	-	-
Scholarships and grants	1,500	1,500	-
Gift from parents	2,000	2,000	-
Student loans	4,500	4,500	-
Total income received	8,000	8,000	-
Taxes withheld on paycheck	-	-	-
Property taxes	-	-	-
Total taxes paid	-	-	-
Savings	-	-	-
Total savings	-	-	-
College Expenses			
Tuition	3,500	3,500	-
* Room and Board	3,200	3,200	-
Computer	-	-	-
Books	400	352	(48)
Supplies	150	95	(55)
Total college expenses	7,250	7,147	(103)
* Apartment rent	-	-	-
* Electricity	-	-	-
* Gas - home	-	-	-
* Water & sewer	-	-	-
* Refuse pick up	-	-	-
* Telephone - home	-	-	-
* Internet	-	-	-
* Cable	-	-	-
* Groceries	-	-	-
Health insurance	48	48	-
Telephone - cell	53	57	4
Auto loan payment	-	-	-
Auto insurance	40	40	-
Auto - gasoline	60	73	13
Auto maintenance	-	-	-
Life insurance	185	185	-
Clothes	-	35	35
Recreation (meals out, etc.)	50	65	15
Christmas gifts	-	-	-
Other	-	-	-
Total other expenses	436	503	67
Net cash balance (cash shortfall)	314	350	36

* If student lives off campus, then substitute these items for the room and board costs paid to the college.

CHAPTER SEVENTEEN
Net Worth Statement

Everyone wants to know the score of the game. Who played well and, of course, who won the game. Sports analysts study the strategies of the coaches and instant replay permits us to see the same play over and over again. Each sport has a season and, at the end of the season, a league champion emerges. Then, the coaches begin to plan for the next season.

Finance is really no different. You want to know your financial score; what is your net worth? You are very interested in how your investments are performing and whether your financial strategies are delivering the results anticipated. The finance season is generally a calendar year (the season lasts all year).

In order to assess where you are financially, you need to prepare a net worth statement. Although a net worth statement can be prepared anytime, you should prepare a net worth statement at least once a year (perhaps as of December 31). This chapter will highlight how to prepare a net worth statement to assist in determining how your finance team did for the current year.

A net worth statement will assist you in consolidating finances by having one list of all of your assets and liabilities. Exhibit 17A provides an example of a net worth statement.

Net Worth Statement. A net worth statement summarizes the value of the things you own (assets) and the amount you owe to other people (liabilities). The value of assets minus liabilities equals net worth at a point in time. If you owe more than the value of your assets, then you have a net deficit. A large net deficit causes people to go into bankruptcy, especially if they cannot make the required monthly payments on the amount they owe.

Date. A net worth statement is prepared as of a particular date, which means that all assets and liabilities are valued as of the date selected. For example, the last day of a month is generally selected as the date for the net worth statement. Try to determine the value of each asset and liability as of the end of the month selected.

Assets. List all of your assets, which include bank accounts, savings accounts, investments, autos, and furniture. Then, assign a value to each item listed as of the date selected to use for the net worth statement. For example, the value to use for bank and savings accounts would be the cash in those accounts as of the end of the month selected. Investments would be valued at the market value listed on the monthly investment statement.

Other assets, such as cars, homes, and furniture, are more difficult to value. Generally, a car would be worth less than the amount paid for the car (a car depreciates and loses value as it gets older). On the other hand, real estate generally is worth more than the amount paid (real estate appreciates and increases in value). Don't get too caught up in trying to get an exact value – an approximate value will generally be sufficient.

Liabilities. The amount of liabilities is generally easier to determine. Monthly statements from creditors will generally indicate how much you owe. Included in liabilities are credit card balances, unpaid utility amounts, and any type of loan (student, auto, and home). The liability amount should be determined at the same date selected to value assets (such as at the end of a month).

Net Worth. Your net worth is equal to your assets minus your liabilities at any point in time. Hopefully, you have a positive number after subtracting liabilities from assets. This would mean that your assets are worth more than the amount of your liabilities and that you are in a good financial position. Your budget would help you to decide how to continue to increase your net worth over time by saving, making investments, etc.

Net Deficit. However, if your liabilities are higher than your assets (called a net deficit), then you have some work to do. If you can make the required monthly payments from your earnings, then you can perhaps reduce the net deficit over time (that is, if more than just interest is paid on loans). Your budget now comes into play to help you to determine how much you can pay each month to reduce the deficit.

If you have student loans, you will probably have a net deficit on your net worth statement because of the money borrowed for your college education. Remember that no payments on student loans are required while you are in college. Therefore, you only need to focus on being able to pay all of your other liabilities currently as promised. Of course, you still want to keep your student loans to a minimum because they must be repaid when you leave college as explained in Chapter Eight on student loans.

NOTES

Net Worth Statement
Key Points

- A net worth statement

  - Lists all of your assets and liabilities
  - Summarizes financial condition at one point in time

- Prepare a net worth statement

  - At least once a year (perhaps as of December 31)
  - Select a date at the end of a month to value assets and to determine the amount of liabilities
  - Assets minus liabilities equals net worth (or net deficit)

- Budgets can help increase net worth or reduce net deficits

NOTES

Exhibit 17A - Example of a Net Worth Statement

Assets

Checking account	400	
Savings account	3,000	
Investment account	1,500	
Cash value of life insurance	500	
Car	8,000	
Furniture	1,000	
Other		
Total Assets		14,400

Liabilities

Credit card A	450	
Credit card B	300	
Student loans	8,000	
Car loans	5,000	
Other		
Total Liabilities		13,750
Net Worth (assets minus liabilities)		650

NOTES

CHAPTER EIGHTEEN
Financial and Personal Records

Baseball fans seem to keep all of their baseball cards forever; you never know how much they may be worth in 25 years. But financial and personal records can quickly accumulate to an unmanageable pile of paper. Therefore, you need a system to sort and retain the required financial and personal records for future use.

Maintaining financial and personal records will save a tremendous amount of time and perhaps a lot of money. Some documents will be needed for a lifetime (birth certificates, life insurance policies, etc.) and other documents will be needed for several years. Setting up a system to maintain these records will not only save time and money, but will save anxiety trying to find records at the last minute.

Your Signature. Read all documents before signing them and always receive a copy of anything you sign. Maintaining a copy of all signed documents will help if there is a later dispute.

Do not rely on another person to explain the terms of an agreement. We don't always listen closely to what is said and may not fully understand the explanation of the terms of an agreement. Further, it may not be what the person said, but what the person didn't say about the terms of the document that is important.

For example, an item may be purchased with zero interest for twelve months. The fine print may state that if the entire balance is not paid within twelve months, then the interest rate will be 21% from the date the item was purchased. Clearly, you would not agree to pay 21% interest. But, if you don't make payment as agreed, you are obligated to pay this high interest rate. Always read the fine print. Also, keep a copy of the sales agreement so you can read the terms of the sales agreement at a later date and understand whether there is a basis for your side of a dispute.

Personal Records. Personal records are records other than financial records. For example, personal records would include birth certificate, diplomas, social security card, passport, college transcripts, certification documents, license documents, marriage certificate, military service records, and estate planning documents. Most of these documents will be considered permanent files.

Financial Records. Basically, a financial record is any document (piece of paper or computer file) that deals with money. Some examples of financial records are bank statements, investment statements, pay stubs, tax returns, loan documents, insurance policies, and titles to cars. Organize financial records by separating them into annual files and permanent files.

Annual Files. Annual files are any documents which pertain to one year, such as checking account statements, credit card statements, investment account statements, retirement plan statements, tax returns, and all documents which support the tax returns. You should maintain these documents by year for easy retrieval if needed in the future. A good way to set up annual files is to use file folders and place them in a file storage box.

You should retain checking account and credit card statements that support tax deductions for at least three years after the income tax return is filed. Discard deposit slips and ATM receipts after the transactions appear on the checking account statement.

Shred monthly and quarterly investment account statements after the annual investment account statement has been verified as accurate.

Retain trade confirmations showing the purchase and sale of mutual funds and stocks for three years after filing the income tax return that reports the sale of the mutual fund or stock.

Shred monthly and quarterly retirement plan statements after you verify the annual retirement plan summary statement as accurate.

Maintain income tax returns and supporting documents for the income tax returns in a separate folder for each year. Keep some of these files for an extended period of time. For example, keep income tax returns forever. Save the supporting documents, such as receipts for a tax deduction, for a minimum of three years after the return is filed.

Retain pay stubs until you verify the totals on Form W-2 (annual wage form provided by your employer) as correct. Verify information including wages, federal income tax withheld, and state income tax withheld. After you are satisfied that the W-2 is correct, shred pay stubs for that year. You will use the W-2 to prepare your income tax returns.

Unless you need utility bills to support a home office deduction for income tax purposes, shred these bills after they have been paid. However, you may wish to keep at least one year of utility bills to compare the current year bill with the prior year bill to determine how you are controlling usage of the utility. By having the prior year utility bills, you can respond to a home buyer's request to provide a summary of the annual utility bills for the home.

Permanent Files. Permanent files are files which you should keep for more than one year (and perhaps for a lifetime), such as birth certificate, marriage certificate, diplomas, social security card, life insurance policies, passport, deed to a home, contracts, and will.

Make a copy of all of the permanent files for quick reference and place the original documents in a safe place, such as a safety deposit box at a bank. You can arrange the copies in a notebook (or notebooks) with an index to the documents. This index also serves as an inventory of the original documents that are in the other location. Exhibit 18A provides a sample permanent file index.

Other Files. Retain receipts for major purchases and warranties for as long as you own the item.

Financial and Personal Records
Key Points

- Maintain financial and personal records to save time

- Read any document before signing the document

- Keep a copy of any document that you sign

- Arrange annual files by year for easy retrieval

- Retain monthly and quarterly statements until annual statements have been verified

- Retain documents that support income tax returns for at least three years after the return is filed

- Prepare an index (inventory) of permanent records

  - Make a copy of permanent records for quick reference
  - Put the originals of permanent records in a safe place

TOPAZ CONSULTING, LLC

Exhibit 18A - Permanent File Index

Page 1 of 2

	Description/Company	Document/ Title/Policy Number	Purchase/ Issue Date	Original Document Location	Copy Location Notebook	Tab
Family Documents						
J	Marriage Certificate			SDB	1	1
H	Birth Certificate			SDB	1	2A
H	Copy of U. S. Passport			SDB	1	2A
H	Social Security Card			SDB	1	2A
W	Birth Certificate			SDB	1	2B
W	Copy of U. S. Passport			SDB	1	2B
W	Social Security Card			SDB	1	2B
J	Jewelry Documents			SDB	1	2C
H	Diploma			Wall	1	3A
H	Transcript			SDB	1	3A
W	Diploma			Wall	1	3B
W	Transcript			SDB	1	3B
H	Certificate			Wall	1	4
W	Certificate			Wall	1	4
	Military Records			SDB	1	5
Estate Planning						
H	Will			SDB	2	1
H	Revocable Trust Agreement			SDB	2	2
H	Irrevocable Trust Agreement			SDB	2	3
H	Durable General Power of Attorney			SDB	2	4A
H	Advance Medical Directive			SDB	2	4B
W	Will			SDB	2	5
W	Revocable Trust Agreement			SDB	2	6
W	Irrevocable Trust Agreement			SDB	2	7
W	Durable General Power of Attorney			SDB	2	8A
W	Advance Medical Directive			SDB	2	8B
	Beneficiary Form					
H	Pension Plan			SDB	2	9A
H	IRA			SDB	2	9B
H	401(K) Plan			SDB	2	9C
W	Pension			SDB	2	10A
W	IRA			SDB	2	10B
W	401(K) Plan			SDB	2	10C

H = Husband, W = Wife, J = Joint
SDB = Safe Deposit Box at Bank

Exhibit 18A - Permanent File Index

Page 2 of 2

	Description/Company	Document/ Title/Policy Number	Purchase/ Issue Date	Original Document Location	Copy Location Notebook	Tab
Homes						
J	Deed, Title Ins.			SDB	3	1A
J	Mortgage			SDB	3	1B
Automobiles						
H	Title			SDB	3	2
W	Title			SDB	3	3
Home Insurance						
J				SDB	4	1
Umbrella Liability						
J				SDB	4	2
Auto Insurance						
J				SDB	4	3
Disability Insurance						
H				SDB	4	4
W				SDB	4	5
Cancer Insurance						
J				SDB	4	6
Life Insurance						
H				SDB	5	1
H				SDB	5	2
W				SDB	5	3
W				SDB	5	4
Retirement Plan Documents						
H	Social Security Statement			SDB	6	1
H	Pension			SDB	6	2
H	401 (K) Plan			SDB	6	3
H	IRA			SDB	6	4
W	Social Security Statement			SDB	6	5
W	Pension			SDB	6	6
W	401 (K) Plan			SDB	6	7
W	IRA			SDB	6	8

H = Husband, W = Wife, J = Joint
SDB = Safe Deposit Box at Bank

NOTES

CHAPTER NINETEEN

Additional Thoughts

Valuable Information. Hopefully, this guide has provided valuable information that will assist you in making informed decisions regarding financial matters. The guide does not provide all of the answers, but rather it provides a starting point to help you seek advice from sources that are knowledgeable about a financial transaction that you may be considering.

Legal Disclosure. Please remember that this guide does not provide accounting, investment, legal, or tax advice.

Professionals – Conflict of Interest. Professionals (bankers and insurance agents) are very knowledgeable about their area of expertise and can provide valuable information to help you make a good decision regarding financial matters.

However, in certain circumstances, a "conflict of interest" may develop between you and the professional. A "conflict of interest" means that the professional may earn more money if you purchase a particular item or service or if you pay a price higher than may be necessary for an item or service.

Professionals only make money when they sell a product or service. For example, life insurance agents don't receive income unless you purchase a life insurance policy and they receive more money if you purchase a more expensive life insurance policy (perhaps more life insurance than you need).

Professionals have ethical standards that must be followed, but their income depends on you making decisions that benefit them and sometimes those decisions may not be in your best interest. Educate yourself on the alternatives available so that you can decide which option is best for you (comparative shopping).

You Can Only Spend It Once. Many people try to use the same income to pay for too many things. For example, you may receive $4,800 for a summer job. First, you must pay taxes on the wages. The $4,800 of wages may only be $4,200 after $600 is withheld for taxes. You make tuition payments costing $3,500, purchase new clothes costing $400, pay $250 for car repairs, and take a much-deserved vacation for $300 (including all the extras that you weren't told about).

Once you do the math, you will have overspent your take-home pay by $250. It is very easy to get caught up in spending. Sometimes, we forget to set priorities about spending our income.

Comparative Shopping. One of the best ways to educate yourself about a transaction is to talk to several people about the transaction. For example, when purchasing a car, talk to several dealers about the features of the car, the price of the car, the dealer fees, and the dealer car loan programs. Also, be sure to talk to several auto insurance agents to get the best auto insurance premium possible (this goes for all types of insurance).

When borrowing money for college, shop several sources to be sure that you are receiving the lowest interest rate with repayment terms that meet your needs. You probably need to defer repayment of the loan until after you complete college.

Education. Educating yourself is the best way to maximize your purchasing power by selecting products and services that meet your needs and give you the best total deal. An excellent time to take personal finance courses is while you are attending college. The information learned in these classes will benefit you throughout your lifetime.

The Internet has become an excellent tool for finding information about the key elements of a transaction, about organizations, and about values of property or services. In addition, newspaper and magazine articles provide useful information.

People who work in an area (such as bankers, real estate agents, car dealers, and insurance agents) provide extremely valuable information on a transaction. They are the experts, but remember they may have a conflict of interest.

Rules Subject to Change. Please note that the rules stated in this guide are subject to change and the current rules should be verified before making a decision about a particular transaction. For example, at the time of the writing of this guide, bank accounts were insured for $100,000 per account by the FDIC. There have been discussions to raise this limit (up to as much as $130,000).

Likewise, rules regarding income taxes are subject to change at any time by Congress. For example, this guide states that interest on a home equity loan or home line of credit is deductible for federal income taxes purposes. Congress has considered eliminating this deduction to reduce the federal deficit. Therefore, if you are deciding between a car loan (interest is not tax deductible) and a home equity loan (interest is tax deductible) to purchase a car, you might change your mind if the home equity loan interest is no longer deductible. Now, your decision would be based on the interest rate and fees only.

Financial to-do List. Suggestions provided in this guide that you decide to implement will take time. A financial to-do list will help you in setting priorities when implementing your financial game plan and can help you complete the steps in a timely manner.

The list should be a "living" list of steps to implement your financial game plan, which means you will complete and remove items from the list, as well as add new items to the list. As you implement the financial game plan, you may discover that additional steps are needed to accomplish your goals or that you modify your goals. You will modify the financial to-do list to incorporate these changes.

Enjoy Life. Enjoy you college years and don't obsess about money or about what you should have done or shouldn't have done. Everyone makes financial mistakes. If you make financial mistakes when you are young, you have plenty of time to recover from them by using what you have learned for future transactions.

Time of Learning. Use this time of learning to establish good financial habits that will last you a lifetime. The finance education that you receive while in college (both in the classroom and everyday experiences) will permit you to enjoy a better life by making wise financial decisions in the future.

May all of your purchases be wise and within your means. Best wishes for a joyous and prosperous life.

Additional Thoughts

Key Points

- This guide provides no accounting, investment, legal, or tax advice

- Professionals may have a conflict of interest

- You can only spend money once

- Be sure to shop before you buy

- Continue to educate yourself about financial matters

- Understand the current rules

- Maintain a financial to-do list of steps to be implemented

- ENJOY LIFE

    - Do not obsess about money and budgets
    - Learn from mistakes

- Use this time of learning to develop good financial habits

NOTES